W9-AGG-455

# GREAT MYSTERIES

# ESP

OPPOSING VIEWPOINTS®

Look for these and other exciting *Great Mysteries: Opposing Viewpoints* books:

# GREAT MYSTERIES

# ESP

## OPPOSING VIEWPOINTS®

## by Michael Arvey

Greenhaven Press, Inc.          San Diego, California

Library of Congress Cataloging-in-Publication Data

Arvey, Michael.
    ESP : opposing viewpoints.

    (Great mysteries)
    Bibliography: p.
    Includes index.
    Summary: Examines ESP and related mysteries, including psychokinesis, clairvoyance, and out-of-body experiences, and discusses the experts' evidence, from scientific experiments to personal experiences.
    1. Extrasensory perception—Juvenile literature.
2. Psychical research—Juvenile literature.
[1. Extrasensory perception.  2. Psychical research]
I. Title.  II. Series: Great mysteries (Saint Paul, Minn.)
BF1321.A78  1989     133.8     88-24316
ISBN 0-89908-057-X

*"When men and women lose the sense of mystery, life will prove to be a gray and dreary business, only with difficulty to be endured."*

*Harold T. Wilkins, author of* Strange Mysteries of Time and Space

# Contents

# Introduction

T his book is written for the curious—those who want to explore the mysteries that are everywhere. To be human is to be constantly surrounded by wonderment. How do birds fly? Are ghosts real? Can animals and people communicate? Was King Arthur a real person or a myth? Why did Amelia Earhart disappear? Did history really happen the way we think it did? Where did the world come from? Where is it going?

*Great Mysteries: Opposing Viewpoints* books are intended to offer the reader an opportunity to explore some of the many mysteries that both trouble and intrigue us. For the span of each book, we want the reader to feel that he or she is a scientist investigating the extinction of the dinosaurs, an archaeologist searching for clues to the origin of the great Egyptian pyramids, a psychic detective testing the existence of ESP.

One thing all mysteries have in common is that there is no ready answer. Often there are *many* answers but none on which even the majority of authorities agrees. *Great Mysteries: Opposing Viewpoints* books introduce the intriguing views of the experts, allowing the reader to participate in their explorations, their theories, and their disagreements as they try to explain the mysteries of our world.

But most readers won't want to stop here. These *Great Mysteries: Opposing Viewpoints* aim to stimulate the reader's curiosity. Although truth is often impossible to discover, the search is fascinating. It is up to the reader to examine the evidence, to decide whether the answer is there—or to explore further.

"Penetrating so many secrets, we cease to believe in the unknowable. But there it sits nevertheless, calmly licking its chops."

H.L. Mencken, American essayist

**One**

# The Mystery of ESP

H ave you ever thought of an old friend you had not seen in a while and then you bumped into her in a store? Or perhaps she called you on the telephone?

Have you ever had a forewarning, either in a dream or when you were awake, of something that would occur in the future?

Have you ever been someplace where you sensed danger?

If any of these things have happened to you, you may have had a flash of ESP, sometimes called the "sixth sense."

The letters *ESP* stand for *extra-sensory perception*. Simply defined, ESP means obtaining or sending knowledge or information without the use of the normal five senses of sight, sound, taste, touch, and smell.

Many forms of ESP may exist. They include:

- *Precognition:* knowledge or perception of future events
- *Retrocognition:* knowledge or perception of past events
- *Telepathy:* nonspoken, mind-to-mind communication

COME

This illustration from an old book shows a man receiving an extrasensory message.

12

> "Precognitions have been noted regularly not only in the literature of psychical research but in that of science itself for more than 2,000 years. The Bible includes a remarkable collection of divinely inspired prophecies and promises."
>
> Don Como, Richard Croy, and Brad Steiger, *Unknown Powers*

> "To compare the modern, publicity-prone prognosticator to the ancient prophets of the Bible is nonsensical. The ancient prophets had messages for their times. Predicting inevitable events was their vehicle for criticizing the social and political order."
>
> Magician-columnist Henry Gordon, *Extra Sensory Deception*

- *Clairvoyance:* perception of objects or events not available to normal vision
- *Clairaudience:* hearing sound not available to normal hearing

There are also a number of closely related phenomena. They involve more than mental activity alone; they include mental impact on *physical* things. These phenomena include:

- *Psychokinesis (also called PK):* "mind over matter"; affecting objects—making them move, for example—by a non-physical means
- *Materialization:* making an object appear, seemingly from nowhere
- *Levitation:* the ability to raise your own body, or something else, into the air without using physical means
- *Out-of-Body Experience:* feeling as though you are outside, or separate from, your body; able to observe your body when separate from it

People have been reporting what we call ESP experiences for a long time. Let's go back and look at some of the history of ESP and notice how, even long ago, it was just as much a mystery as it is today.

Since the beginning of recorded history, people

Opposite page: Pythia, the ancient oracle of Delphi. She made many complicated and obscure prophecies. Left: King Croesus, who lost his kingdom when he misinterpreted an oracle.

have sought out those who had access to information or knowledge not available through ordinary channels. The advice and interpretations of prophets, priests, diviners, medicine men and women, shamans, seers, and oracles have been sought out by people at all levels of society.

In ancient Greece, for example, kings often consulted a priest or priestess before making important decisions. Such people would relay divine messages from a god to the kings. Sometimes the message was not perfectly clear. For example, Herodotus, the Greek historian, wrote that King Croesus of Lydia once consulted an oracle, a priest or priestess who made predictions about the future. Croesus wanted information before he began a military campaign against Persia 2600 years ago. The oracle's message was that King

According to the Bible, Joseph correctly interpreted the Pharoah's dreams, thereby saving Egypt from destruction.

Croesus would destroy a great empire. Croesus assumed the doomed empire was that of his enemies, the Persians, so he launched his attack. Unfortunately for King Croesus, it was his own troops that were crushed and destroyed. The oracle had been right—but it was the great empire of Lydia that was destroyed.

Prophets and their prophecies pop up in many of the world's religious texts, the Bible among them. For instance, Joseph in the Old Testament interpreted a king's dreams. The king believed Joseph's interpretations and acted on them, saving the country from a potential famine.

Interestingly enough, the old kings and their prophets have a counterpart in today's presidents with their advisors and committees! And can't we just imagine busy world leaders sometimes wishing they could consult an oracle or two? In fact, it is reported that Franklin D. Roosevelt did indeed visit with psychic Jeane Dixon a couple of times during his terms as president of the United States. As recently as 1988 President Ronald Reagan is said to have based some of his decisions on the advice of an astrologer.

## Ancient India

Accounts of psychic or supernormal activity have been reported all over the world. In India, for example, stories abound of levitating saints, people having glorious visions, and yogis who can be in two places at once. A text survives from ancient India called *The Yoga Sutras of Patanjali*. *Yoga* means "union"; *sutras* means "threads of thought." This book is an early manual of instruction for meditation. Among the sutras, or teachings, that Patanjali devised were instructions for attaining *siddhis,* or psychic powers.

Today, Patanjali's system for developing psychic powers has been revived. The Transcendental Meditation organization offers courses that teach these techniques. The organization claims that, with practice, *psi* (another word for psychic) abilities can be perfected.

Franklin Roosevelt, one American president who is said to have consulted a psychic about some of his presidential decisions.

Current researchers are investigating that claim. What if Patanjali was right? Were the ancients aware of mysteries and possibilities that we only recently have started to reawaken to?

Divinatory arts (practices to obtain messages or insights from a source beyond oneself) have been with us for a long time. Practitioners of these arts have used unusual methods to obtain knowledge of the past, present, and future. These methods have involved the use of shells, bones, sticks, leaves, and other natural objects. Gypsies, for example, are said to have been able to interpret or "read" the shapes of tea leaves that remained in the bottom of teacups. Gypsies also made popular the Tarot, a fortune-telling deck of cards.

Even today, some people in Louisiana are reported to practice divination with eggs. The procedure is this: The "reader" breaks open raw eggs and reads the way the yolks and whites separate. The reader answers the seeker's questions by interpreting the "pictures" or shapes that form in the eggs.

What does all this have to do with ESP? A lot. What is commonly called ESP today has roots more

ancient than history.

Until people started understanding more about ESP, it was associated with the occult (secret lore), the supernatural, magic, and "hocus-pocus." In short, the unexplainable. And anything that cannot be explained often causes fear and condemnation. How have ESP and other psychic phenomena come to be regarded more and more seriously by scientists and lay people alike?

One writer, Jan Ehrenwald, offers three explanations: One, so much seemingly respectable research on ESP has accumulated that it cannot be ignored. Two, the growing number of reported psychic occurrences cannot be ignored. And three, changing attitudes in modern physics and philosophy are affect-

A medium tries to gather extrasensory information from a glove.

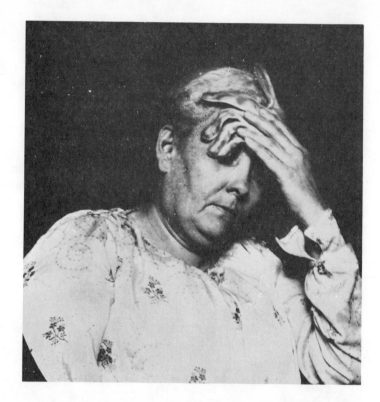

ing attitudes toward ESP. For these reasons, scientists and the public continue to probe the mysteries of ESP. People want to know if it really exists, how it happens, and whether it can be harnessed to help direct their own lives.

## ESP and Controversy

ESP is a controversial subject. Arguments about it have gone on ever since the Society for Psychical Research was founded in England in 1882. One commentator, Ethel Grodzins Romm, wrote: "In fortune-telling land, the proverbial shoe always fits." What she means is that, in her opinion, people who profess to be psychics will say whatever is necessary to sound reliable. However, another writer, Martin Gardner, stated in *Time* magazine: "Modern science should indeed arouse in all of us a humility before the immensity of the unexplained and a tolerance for crazy hypotheses." In other words, Gardner means that people should be more receptive to what they don't understand.

Still, the questioning goes on. Just as modern technology has been exploring outer space, so has it been exploring inner space—the mind. ESP is a part of what is being explored. Now let's see how science and ESP have fared together.

"International activities in the field of parapsychological research have reached a high point."

Author Martin Ebon, *The Psychic Reader*

"Today ESP is no nearer to being established than it was a hundred years ago."

Professor of psychology, C.E.M. Hansel, in *A Skeptic's Handbook of Parapsychology*

# Two

# Science and ESP: Do Opposites Attract?

L ike a poorly matched couple, the scientific community and the ESP community have had a long rocky relationship. They've bickered and tossed accusations at one another, and each has professed to be right about its claims.

In the 1930s, Dr. J.B. Rhine of Duke University in North Carolina initiated the first serious attempts to study ESP. In fact, it was he who coined the term *extra-sensory perception*. Rhine set up seemingly controlled laboratory conditions and proceeded to conduct experiments. Note that in science, no experiment is considered conclusive unless it can be repeated again and again with the same results. Dr. Rhine hoped to achieve this through a statistical approach. In this way, he would verify the existence of ESP.

## Zener Cards

One experiment he devised used Zener cards, named after the scientist who designed them. Each card is blank on one side and has a symbol printed on the other. There are five symbols: a cross, a circle, a star, a square, and wavy lines. Rhine's test was simple: People would be asked to identify the symbols on randomly selected cards without seeing the

Opposite page: Professor Hans Bender, a psychical researcher in Germany, tests a young woman for ESP.

Zener cards used in ESP tests.

cards. The deck has twenty-five cards, and each symbol is printed on five cards. Thus, subjects had a one-in-five chance of being correct. Rhine believed that if people tested had more correct answers (hits) than could be expected from mere chance and guesswork, it would be an indication of ESP at work. So, out of 250 answers, fifty hits (one-fifth of the total answers) would indicate chance success. Seventy or more hits would indicate that ESP might be involved. Since the odds of hitting 80 cards out of 250 were 50,000-to-1, that would be definite proof of ESP.

After conducting thousands of tests, Rhine believed the results showed that more than guesswork was involved. In fact, one of his "star subjects," Adam Linzmeyer, correctly named 119 out of 300 cards—twice as many correct answers as someone would get by chance!

Rhine and his followers also experimented with psychokinesis, or PK. They tested to see if subjects could willfully affect the way dice fell when rolled. Results here too indicated that psychic powers might be real.

Much of Rhine's work has since been challenged by some critics who charge that there were instances of deceit and experimental errors. One criticism was that the subjects could see through the Zener cards. Also, Rhine's outstanding results have never been duplicated by other researchers.

In a recent book, *ESP and Parapsychology*, C.E.M. Hansel notes that "a great deal of experimental work has failed to provide a clear case for the existence of ESP." But he also says that "subjects trying to guess targets have obtained scores that cannot be attributed to chance." In other words, something was happening but no one could define *what*.

The problems researchers have found in studying the existence of ESP are staggering. Those conducting experiments must attempt to eliminate all possibility of trickery and all possible influences from the experimenter; they must establish strictly controlled testing conditions; and they must filter out mere guesswork.

Moreover, D. Scott Rogo, in *Our Psychic Potentials*, contends that ESP is an unconscious process. It rarely announces itself under normal conditions. The demanding conditions of an experiment might make it even more elusive.

Charles Honorton, a former psi researcher at Maimonides Hospital in Brooklyn, New York, agrees. He theorizes that ESP impressions become suppressed by regular activities of the mind and body. If Rogo and Honorton are right, this could account for

Professor S.G. Soal, a mathematician and psychic researcher, devised these animal cards to use in ESP tests instead of the traditional Zener cards.

Right: An ESP experiment. The woman behind the screen is trying to determine, using ESP, which cards the man on the left is laying down. Below: A scorecard for this and other ESP tests that use Zener cards. The circled responses are correct. On all but the second test, the results shown here are much higher than average, suggesting ESP ability at work.

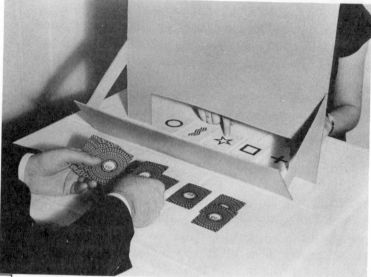

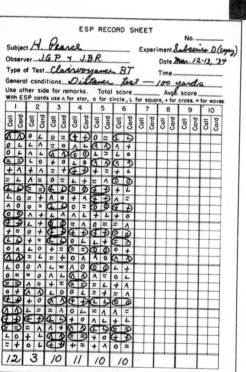

research not being able to come to terms with ESP.

Science values logic and objectivity. But some writers say that ESP is a creature of dreams, intuition, and the unconscious. Science values control. ESP is most dramatic when it happens spontaneously. Hence, ESP is difficult to study. It contradicts the logic of science. Shawn Robbins, in *The Confessions of a Professional Psychic*, declares that the "process of making predictions is illogical and beyond scientific analysis at this time." Thus the problem: Scientific methods don't seem appropriate for studying ESP.

## Remote Viewing and the *Ganzfeld*

Two well-known methods of testing for ESP, however, are said to have shown good results. One is called remote viewing. In this kind of experiment, a subject is asked to clairvoyantly see and describe a distant target area chosen by an experimenter. The subject has no way of knowing what has been selected as the target. Experimenters think that if the subject describes details of a chosen target fairly accurately, it indicates ESP.

Researchers in remote viewing claim their success rate is high, but opponents of remote viewing aren't so sure. One critic, Ethel Grodzins Romm, believes that laboratory tests on remote viewing are "worthless." She gives an example: "To simulate a winter climate, a room was draped with white fabric. For several minutes, someone poured ice cubes down the shivering back of the soaked, suffering 'sender.' One 'receiver' reported 'white' and was promptly judged ESPed, telepathic, and so on." Romm's complaint is that many different words might have described the event, and many of them could have been better than "white." Why not "miserable" or "icy" or "wet," she asks.

*Ganzfeld* tests are another way to test clairvoyance. *Ganzfeld* is a German word meaning "homogeneous" or "same field." In *ganzfeld* testing, a subject is placed in an artificially induced state of sensory and informational deprivation. Typically, the subject's eyes are carefully covered to block out all light. Earphones sending "white noise," a kind of low-volume, monotonous static sound, are placed over the subject's ears to keep out normal sounds from the surrounding environment. The subject's mind then, without external stimulation, creates its own information in the form of dream-like images or hallucinations, perhaps with ESP.

In Charles Honorton's first *ganzfeld* experiment, thirty subjects were instructed to report on their thoughts, feelings, and images for a thirty-five minute period. In another room, an experimenter concentrated on a picture or series of pictures. He would try to mentally "send" scenes to the subjects.

D. Scott Rogo writes that nearly half of the subjects showed some indication of ESP. One subject, targeted with a series of U.S. Air Force Academy scenes, described "an airplane floating over the clouds . . . a five-pointed star . . . an airplane pointing down." Her description very closely resembled the pictures viewed by the experimenter. ESP? Paul

"ESP is a real psychological phenomenon."

R.A. McConnell, *ESP Curriculum Guide*

"Personally, I do not accept ESP for a moment, because it does not make sense."

D.O. Hebb, *Journal of Personality*

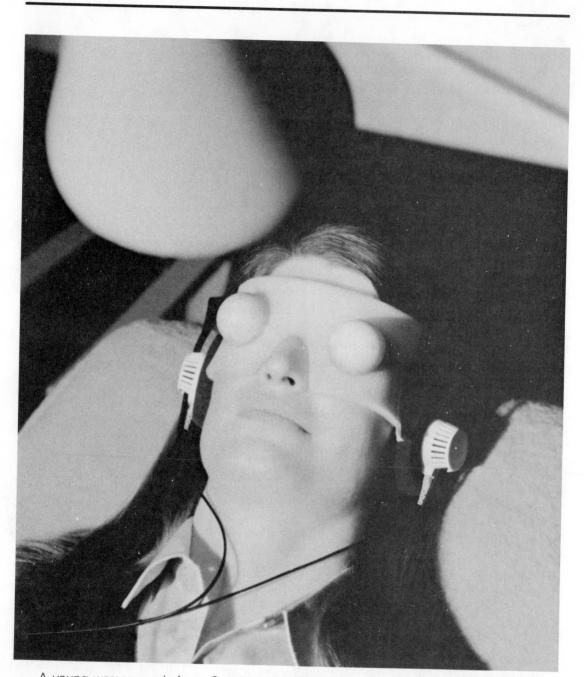

A young woman ready for a *Ganzfeld* test. Her senses have been neutralized: Her eyes are covered; ''white noise,'' similar to the sound of the ocean, is playing in her headphones; a red light bathes the room; and she is lying on a comfortable couch. All of this is supposed to relax her, deprive her mind of distracting sensory input, and make her receptive to mental messages. In another room, a partner will concentrate on photographs and attempt to send her mental pictures.

Chance thinks not. There is "no way of knowing when a correct answer came from psychic insight and when it was just a lucky stab," he insists.

Yet Honorton, analyzing his data, discovered that some of the subjects described the scenes before they were even sent. Were the subjects tuning into the sender's mind as he or she set up the pictures? Rogo doesn't think so: "It looked more as though their minds had picked up this information directly from the reels" of pictures. "But," he questions, "was it really the imagery induced by the *ganzfeld* that led to the success of Honorton's experiment? Or was the state of mind produced by sensory isolation the reason for the outcome of the project?" In other words, what was most important, the receptivity of the subjects, the isolated environment, or the pictures? These questions have not been answered.

### ESP: Relaxation or Concentration?

The differences between remote viewing and *ganzfeld* tests lead to an important question. Russell Targ and Keith Harary, in *The Mind Race*, remark that remote viewing stresses the use of the subject's full

Ted Serios claims he can make photographs with mental energy alone. He concentrates hard on a mental image and points a camera at himself. He claims that when the film is processed, the photos are of his mental images. Below left: A mental photo by Ted Serios. Below right: Ted Serios.

An ESP experiment with remote sending. The man (opposite page, right) concentrates on one of the Zener card symbols. He attempts to mentally transmit his choice to the young woman on the near right. She focuses on the Zener cards, attempting to perceive his mental image. The woman in the middle records on a scoresheet (similar to the one on page 24) the image the man sends and the image the young woman receives. The scoresheet will later be analyzed to determine whether or not ESP may have been present.

attention and concentration. The *ganzfeld*, on the other hand, requires a state of relaxation. Which, then, is more conducive to ESP?

Assuming ESP is a creature of dreams and the unconscious, mightn't it be more naturally associated with relaxation? Some people believe so.

D. Scott Rogo says, "If one is looking for a solution to the ESP mystery, this certainly might be a critical clue." According to Rogo, parapsychologist Rhea White was first to suggest that relaxation may enhance ESP phenomena. White had wondered why it was that the great psychics of the past seemed to do better than present-day psychics tested in laboratories. She discovered that many psychics, to set up the right conditions for a psi experience, began by relaxing.

There are speculations that relaxation may be the *key* to ESP. There are several reasons for this, says Zak Martin in *How To Develop Your ESP*. One, when the body relaxes, the mind relaxes. As a result, he states, the mind, or consciousness, may expand. This means the mind becomes more aware of whatever

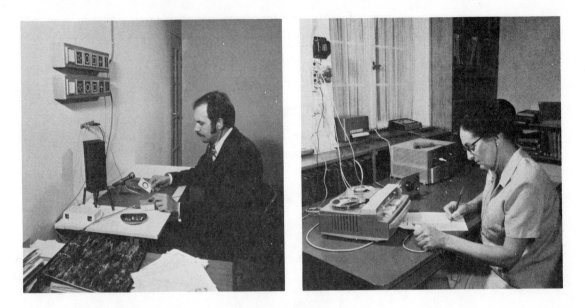

there is to be aware of. Two, when the mind is relaxed, it becomes clearer, more alert. Clairvoyance means ''clear vision.'' Relaxation may promote such vision. Three, with relaxation, tension and stress are released, mentally and physically. This may allow psi channels to open up. And four, when the mind calms down and shakes off its mental clutter, it may be more able to receive psychic impressions.

## Brain Research: Now You See It, Now You Don't?

Modern brain reseach confirms that relaxed states of the mind and body produce brain waves known as alpha waves. Studies trying to relate ESP and brain waves, however, haven't been conclusive. No clear and simple relationship seems to exist between the two.

Research does point out that the two hemispheres, or halves, of the brain serve different functions. (Actually, science tells us that the halves of our brains are really two separate brains!) The left brain is the logical, analytical, reasoning side; the right brain is the artistic, intuitive, dreaming side. Researchers ask: Is the right brain the home of ESP?

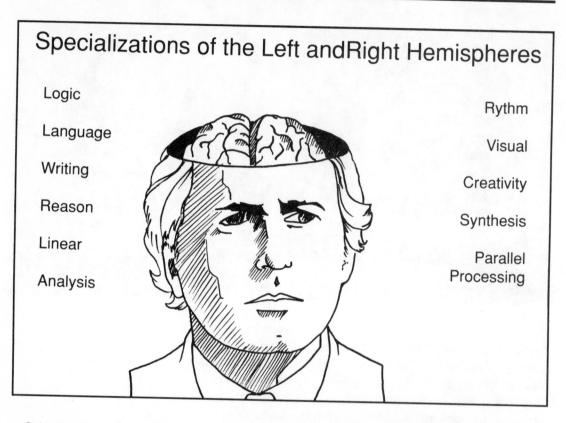

## Specializations of the Left andRight Hemispheres

Logic

Language

Writing

Reason

Linear

Analysis

Rythm

Visual

Creativity

Synthesis

Parallel
Processing

Scientists today believe the brain's two halves control different kinds of functions. Does the right brain control our ESP?

Jan Ehrenwald in *The ESP Experience* writes: "If a skeptic is inclined to dismiss the quest for psi phenomena as a wild goose chase, he is likely to consider the search for the actual habitat of the rare birds as an even more foolhardy undertaking. Yet there can be no doubt that psi phenomena have a foothold somewhere in our neurophysiological organization [nervous system].'' Ehrenwald is saying that locating the *source* of ESP is even more difficult than finding ESP itself, but both probably originate in the brain.

John Fairley and Simon Welfare, authors of *Arthur C. Clarke's World of Strange Powers,* pose two questions regarding this: If psi phenomena do exist and originate in the right brain, how did they get there, and can they be gotten out?

Richard Broughton suggests that psi ability may

have been what humans used to communicate with before they developed spoken languages. Hence, the ability is still there, but has withered through disuse.

Broughton writes: "Just for the fun of it, perhaps we should give the so-called minor hemisphere [right brain] a better chance in the ESP game." The reality is that no research has proved that ESP, if it exists, is in one side of the brain or the other.

## ESP and Energy

Another research problem is this: What kind of energy does ESP use? Does it operate on energy we

"After decades of research and experiments, the parapsychologists are not one step closer to acceptable scientific proof of psychic phenomena."

Daniel Cohn, *Time*

"It is no coincidence that those most skeptical of ESP research are almost invariably those who are least acquainted with the facts."

Mathematician Dr. Samuel George Soal

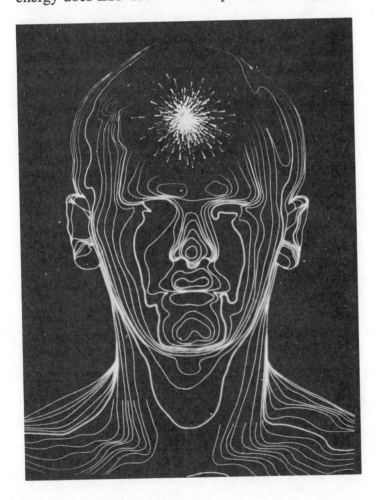

If ESP exists, what kind of energy does it use? Can the energy be harnessed and put to use?

know about, such as electromagnetism or gravity? Or does it operate on energy we have yet to discover? Do all minds have access to a psychic energy that can fuel ESP?

Author Nils O. Jacobson suggests that the brain may act as a kind of electrical transformer converting physical energy to psychic energy.

Wild speculation? Not if reports about a Czech inventor, Robert Pavlita, are accurate. He claims to have invented psychotronic devices—generators able to gather and store psychic energy. Pavlita holds the small generators to his head to capture psychic energy. Then, after the energy is stored, it can be released to produce psi phenomena. He points the charged-up generators at small objects and they move! If this is true, can the brain also act as a transformer, as Jacobson suggests?

## Mental Radio

In *Mental Radio*, published in 1930, writer Upton Sinclair documented experiments he performed

Author Upton Sinclair and his wife Mary experimented with telepathy. They became convinced that ESP worked something like radio waves do. Below right: Upton Sinclair. Below left: The top drawing is an image Sinclair "sent" to his wife. The bottom one is the sketch she made in response to the mental image she received.

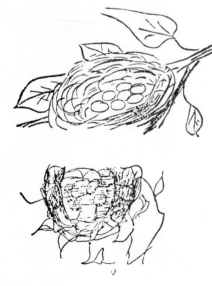

Gladys Wright (above) was a midwife in rural England. One bitter winter night she got a strong feeling that one of her patients needed her. Mrs. Goodwin was not due to give birth for more than a week, yet Nurse Wright's feeling was so strong that she went out into the cold night and drove the treacherous roads to the Goodwin house. She arrived to find the phones out of order and Mrs. Goodwin in hard labor. The baby, now an adult, was born only a few hours later. The Goodwin family is pictured above left.

with his wife Mary. She successfully reproduced drawings that Upton and others mentally sent to her. As a result, the Sinclairs speculated that the mind acts as a kind of radio, sending signals as well as receiving them.

Possible? Not if research is correct. If telepathy does operate on a radio-like principle, then messages should diminish in intensity over long distances. That has not been the case. It has been reported in one case that telepathy occurred at a distance of 5,000 miles.

For example, writer Martin Ebon recounts the following story taken from the files of psychic researcher, Louisa Rhine, wife of J.B. Rhine. One of Rhine's subjects reported:

My very young daughter was working with the United Nations in Korea before the Korean War. At that time, people hardly knew where Korea was on the map. She was the only woman traveling around on trains with a group of men, setting up election booths, getting ready for the free election.

One morning I woke up with a slight feeling

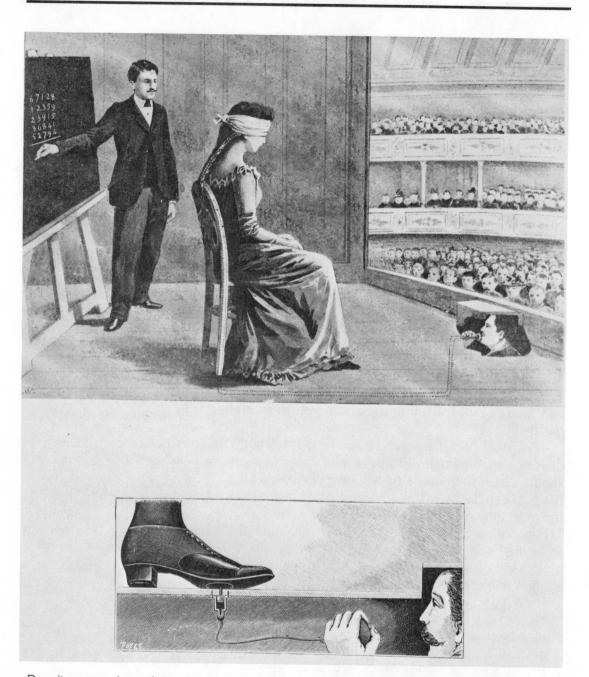

Despite many dramatic and poignant stories that seem to prove ESP's existence, a lot of people don't believe in it. They think that most ESP episodes can be explained by luck, coincidence, or fraud. The pictures above show a turn-of-the century stageshow supposedly demonstrating clairvoyance but actually tricking the audience.

"Alice might call me today," although I knew that this was a very long distance telephone call. This feeling persisted through the day and I did a lot of things and ran around being made very restless by it. Late in the afternoon, I stopped in at the house of her grandmother who was ill and blue and begged me to stay to dinner with her and help her pass the evening. "No, Mother, I can't. I have the idea that Alice will call me tonight." And Mother, although she was stiff about most things, said, "If you feel so, then she will call." I went home.

Well, when I got inside my front door, the knowledge of her call hit me like a thunderbolt. It was not guesswork, or hoping, or wishful thinking; it was pure, direct knowledge. I was unable to eat and for some reason was exhausted. I went to bed finally, and thinking I might go to sleep, I left the light on near me. I fell heavily asleep. At 11 P.M. the telephone rang (I of course knew what it was) and it took twenty minutes for the various controls to connect up with one another and then came the little voice so clear, "Hello, Mother—are you surprised?"

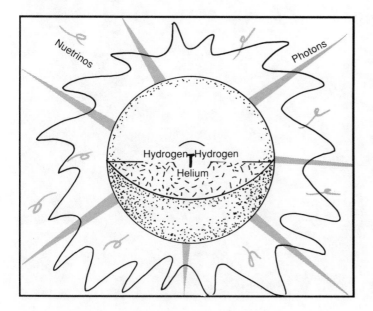

Studies of both science and ESP reveal mysterious events in each. Some of the most puzzling events in science relate to invisible, subatomic particles. Here we see an artist's view of neutrinos, wild, tiny particles that behave in apparently random fashion. Neutrinos occur when hydrogen nuclei collide, react, and become helium nuclei. This reaction produces photons (tiny particles that appear to be light) and neutrinos.

The point about the sure knowledge is the greater because Alice herself did not know that she was going to call me that evening. It turned out that someone else who was going to call America couldn't do so for some reason and Alice at the last minute substituted her call. In short, I knew long before she did that she would call.

It seems that with ESP, distance makes no difference.

## ESP and Physics

Lately, investigators into the worlds of ESP and sub-atomic particles (portions of matter that are smaller than atoms) have noticed a relationship between the two worlds: Unexplained and bizarre events occur in both. The mystery is that these events in some ways look similar.

Will science ever be able to solve the mysteries of ESP?

Physicists have isolated sub-atomic particles that behave randomly, without any pattern. One physicist describes the situation this way: "It's psychedelic [mind-boggling] confusion." Strangest of all are neutrinos, particles that move at the speed of light and are believed to be able to pass through physical matter, like ghosts walking through walls. In short, these particles may be pure energy itself.

Along these lines, are there such things as psi particles? According to V.A. Firsoff, a British astronomer, the answer is yes. He calls them *mindons* and believes they may be related to neutrinos. Another scientist uses the term *psychon* for mindons. In 1965, Adrian Dobbs, a mathematician, theorized that *psitrons* exist and behave like neutrinos. To Dobbs, telepathy is feasible because the brain could generate psitrons that scatter and carry telepathic messages to the brains of people on the receiving end of these psitrons.

## No Conclusions

Despite some similarities between the worlds of science and ESP, the two fields are having a hard time coming to grips with each other. Some experiments indicate that ESP exists, but to scientists the results are inconclusive. In the next chapter, we'll consider some reported ESP experiences and some theories and viewpoints about them.

"I believe that available evidence of ESP is sufficient to establish its reality beyond all reasonable doubt."

R.A. McConnell, *ESP Curriculum Guide*

"After 100 years of research, not a single individual has been found who can demonstrate ESP to the satisfaction of independent investigators."

Professor of psychology C.E.M. Hansel, *ESP and Parapsychology*

Three

# Tricks of the Unconscious

Opposite page: One
mother's precognition told
her that something bad had
happened to her son.

The day my son died in a tragic accident I was
working in an office as a secretary. It was summer,
My son was at a ranch 200 miles away. I found myself
extremely jittery and unable to concentrate on my
work. I told the other girl in the office that I didn't
know what was wrong with me but that I felt that
I just *had* to talk to my son. Our employer was out
and I told her I was going to place a call from his
office, putting the charges on my home phone, and
see if I could possibly reach him [her son]. I called
but was unable to get someone to get him to the
phone. I left word to try to get him to the phone and
call me. I paced the floor all day and when I arrived
home I was shaking so badly I couldn't eat and my
brother was alarmed at my condition. I called the
ranch again but got no response. I couldn't calm
down. I even took a warm bath to try to relax—I found
myself praying and praying—I couldn't sleep. I sat
in the living [room] that night in a chair by the window, reading the Bible and other things to try to quiet
me. It started to rain and a sudden terrific bolt of
lightning hit the tree outside the window and split
it in two. I jumped up and yelled "B---!" [her son's
name]. I didn't know why—or what that had to do
with anything—only that it happened to be a part of

the experience.

At about 1 a.m. or so there was a knock on the door. The director of the ranch stood there. He said he just could not call me and give me the news over the phone—a tractor my son had been riding on had turned over and he had been killed. He had driven all the way—about a 4-hr. drive—to tell me of the news.

What I don't understand is the tremendous feeling of desperately wanting to talk to my son that day—the terrific build-up of jitters and tension—throughout the day—before it happened. The accident happened at 8 p.m. (in summer, it is still quite light . . . at that time of day). Was it the sense of impending danger? . . . No one knows there is impending danger in a *sudden accident*. Was it planned to happen or meant to happen? Was my urge to talk to him an effort to save him—from something I didn't (nor did anyone) know was going to happen?—or the desire to talk to him—one last time? I don't have the answers. All I can say is this is a true experience.

Thus ends writer Loyd Auerbach's story of one mother's ESP experience with her son, and sadly so. But not all ESP experiences are tragic. Here is another story Auerbach reports:

A teenage girl was walking to her father's tailoring shop one afternoon and she passed by a large and unusual car, which she recognized to be a converted hearse. The large black automobile was parked across the street from the town drug store. Although there was no one near the car at the time, her intuition led her to believe that two men had driven the car into town and that these men intended to rob the drug store.

When she arrived at her father's shop, she told her father and some other men who were present of her feelings. They, of course, laughed at her prediction. But she insisted that she was right and added that there would be a thunderstorm in a half hour (at that time it was clear and sunny) and at that time the drug store would be robbed. Sure enough, about a half hour later in the midst of a sudden thunder shower, the drug store was robbed. What's more, one

Sometimes people claim to foresee events. Often they are not believed. This happened to the teenager who told her father that there would be a robbery.

of the men who had overheard the girl's story had gone to a druggist to have another laugh over the silly premonition. He was also robbed and lost $300.

## Does the Future Exist Now?

Both the mother and the teenage girl in these two stories had *premonitions*, knowledge or feelings about events that haven't yet happened. Premonitions have been reported by the thousands throughout the world. This suggests that they're common experiences and that a lot of people may have psychic abilities. Yet the central question that critics ask is how can the future be known when it doesn't yet exist? Common sense tells us that we can't foresee the future because it hasn't happened. Therefore, are prophets merely liars who make up stories that may or may not come true?

Another question critics of ESP ask is, if they are real, where do such messages come from? From our imaginations? From other people's minds? From the gods? From the dead?

Writer Loyd Auerbach asks, "If I predict an event, then act to stop the event from happening (and succeed in stopping it), where did the information come

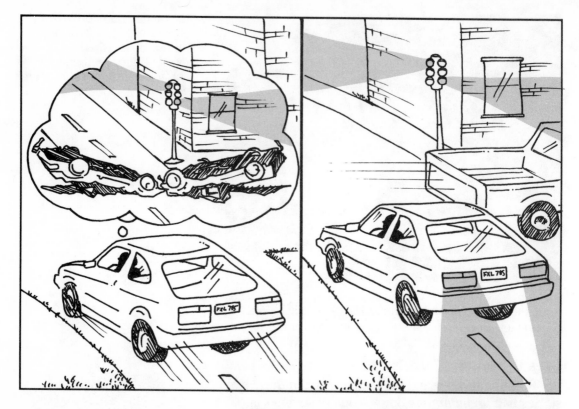

If you predict an accident and manage to prevent it, was your prediction right—or wrong?

from? How could I predict something that didn't happen? Let me give you an example. Let's say I'm driving along and I have a premonition of being in an accident when I enter the next intersection. I jam on the brakes before I go through the green light and suddenly a truck drives straight through the red light and right through where my car could have been. I don't have the accident because I obeyed the precognitive [predictive] warning, *therefore my prediction is untrue*." (Italics added.) The predicted accident did not happen.

Auerbach also writes that some people have explained the relationship between ESP and the future in this way: "The future is a series of probabilities [likely to come true] and that what precognition [premonition] may do is get information from the most likely future to occur, enabling us to make a decision that either brings it into being, or stops it from happening.''

As we can see, the way ESP works in regard to time involves some difficult concepts. Let's look at more cases and theories that relate to the questions we've raised and see if we can't gain a better understanding of what's going on.

## Two Presidents

In her book *Beyond Explanation?* Jenny Randles describes startling incidents of premonition related to the deaths of Presidents Abraham Lincoln and John F. Kennedy: ''On April 1, 1860, Lincoln told his lawyer of a dream he'd had: 'There seemed to be a death-like stillness about me; then I heard subdued sobs, as if a number of people were weeping.' Lincoln told his lawyer that he wandered about the White House until he saw a 'corpse wrapped in funeral vestments.' And, in turn, was told in his dream that the corpse was the President.'' On April 14, 1860, Lincoln was assassinated.

It's also said that in 1960, a hundred years later, President Kennedy had a feeling he would die in office. Hours before he was shot in Dallas on November 22, 1963, he said to his wife and to an aide: ''If somebody wants to shoot me from a window with a rifle, nobody can stop it. So why worry about it?''

Randles writes that numerous premonitions about Kennedy's death occurred. One was experienced by Anne Phillips, a British housewife: ''The night before Kennedy was shot, she had a dream in which she 'saw' the U.S. President driving in a car when three holes suddenly appeared in his head.''

Well-known psychic Jeane Dixon is also reported to have had a premonition about Kennedy. Dixon said that she had a vision in 1952 of Kennedy outside the White House along with the numbers 1960 and a dark cloud over the White House. Dixon said she knew that

Author Jenny Randles has reported on many incidents of premonition involving famous people.

President Abraham Lincoln dreamed of his own death two weeks before it happened.

the man elected in 1960 would die.

Mere coincidences? Or could Lincoln's dream have come from some place other than his imagination? D. Scott Rogo points out that no one has ever satisfactorily explained why such remarkable coincidences happen.

## An Eternal River of Thought?

Randles believes the answer has to do with the *collective unconscious*. Psychic Edgar Cayce described the collective unconscious as a "vast river of thought flowing through eternity, fed by the collective mental activity of mankind since its beginning." It "is accessible to anyone who develops his [or her] own psychic faculties to such a degree as to be able to draw from, as well as feed into, this river of thought." In other words, the collective unconscious could be likened to a river made up of individual drops of water. Each drop by itself is like an individual person's mind. Put together, all the drops make a collective whole, one large river or mind. Hence, if a person could tap into that river, he or she could have a lot more knowledge available than just what comes from his or her individual mind. This could explain where ESP

President John F. Kennedy (above) also is said to have had a premonition of his death (left).

comes from.

Since the collective unconscious is said to be everywhere at the same time, information and events could be transferable across time and space.

Perhaps you read science fiction books. If so, you know that science fiction writers like to play around with fantastic ideas that might or might not be true. Loyd Auerbach states, "Science fiction writers have played for years with the idea of parallel worlds, universes in another space-time that may be anything from extremely similar to our own, to vastly different. In the light of such a . . . bizarre notion, when psi [ESP] information goes wrong, it may be that the information is being received from a present or future world just the slightest bit different from our own,

Psychic Jeane Dixon predicted President Kennedy's death. She writes an astrology column that is published in newspapers all over the country. She has also acted as a psychic advisor to many famous people.

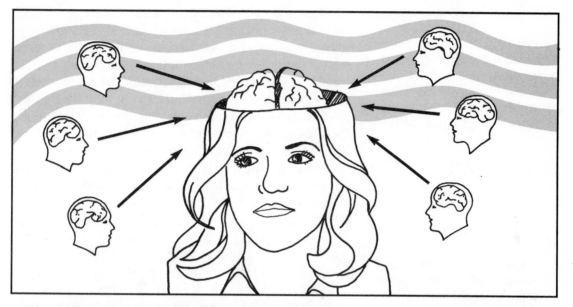

with similar situations and different outcomes."

Along these lines, Randles describes another startling case of premonition. It concerns Jules Verne and two of his novels which were published in the mid-1800s. *From the Earth to the Moon* and its sequel *Round the Moon* are novels involving "airships." Randles writes that Verne's launch site for his airships was in Florida, near Cape Canaveral. The space travel technology that Verne envisioned became true—we've sent men to the moon. Randles summarizes what happens: "In Verne's story an oxygen explosion prevents the spaceship *Columbiad* from landing on the moon, so instead it has to use a remarkable 'slingshot' tactic to catapult itself back to Earth. It crashes into the sea, and its fortunate crew are rescued by a ship in the Pacific."

In 1970, Apollo 13 was launched on a journey to the moon. NASA named it the *Columbia*. During its voyage, an oxygen tank exploded, preventing the ship from landing. The crew devised a "slingshot" tactic similar to Verne's and got the *Columbia* back to Earth. It was rescued out of the Pacific Ocean.

Does ESP come from the collective unconscious? This is described by some as a sort of mental pool that everyone's mind is part of.

Those unwilling to accept the existence of ESP call this sort of thing a coincidence. But Randles explains it as *psychic parallelism:* "By some psychic means the writer creates a fiction which later parallels reality." What is that psychic means? Do some writers have very active imaginations, or do they have ESP?

ESP, Randles would say. She backs this up with theories about two major ways in which we experince life. One is the ordinary, conscious way—being awake and performing everyday activities. The other is when we experience and receive information through our dreams or through the unconscious part of our minds, which can be active even though we're awake. This is how people can know of future events. The psychologist Carl Jung called this *synchronicity.*

To explain this synchronicity, Randles uses an example of swinging pendulums. Though they may be started at different speeds, she notes, "they will gradually share their momentum and end up swinging in harmony." Randles believes that, at certain times, two people might have the same thought at the same time. Or a person's mind might simply tune in to possible future events. For example, Jules Verne's mind could have been unconsciously tuning in to America's future space program that launched men to the moon.

Another writer who seemed to have unusual prescience, or knowledge of things before they happen, was Morgan Robertson, who wrote sea novels in the late 1800s. In his book *The Wreck of the Titan*, he tells a story about a ship that strikes an iceberg in the Atlantic Ocean and sinks with a heavy loss of life. In 1912, the famous *Titanic* sank in the exact same circumstances. ESP? Randles would offer a definite yes.

### Flight 191

Consider another remarkable story as reported in *Arthur C. Clarke's World of Strange Powers*: For ten days in 1979, David Booth of Cincinnati, Ohio, was obsessed with a terrible, recurring dream. In the

More than one hundred years ago, author Jules Verne wrote space exploration stories that have remarkable parallels to today's space experiments. Did Verne have ESP?

dream, he saw a plane crash. He described a three-engined jet that rolled over in the air before it smashed into the ground. Booth stated, "It was like I was standing there watching the whole thing, like watching television."

Booth called authorities at Cincinnati Airport control and at the Federal Aviation Administration. Although the officials took Booth seriously, they finally decided there wasn't anything they could do. They felt that they couldn't cancel all flights or inspect every plane just because of a dream.

On Friday, May 25, an American Airlines jet, Flight 191, crashed at Chicago's O'Hare Airport on take-off. The jet, a DC-10, had three engines. Two hundred seventy-three people died. Photographs taken by a bystander show the jet rolling over just before it crashed.

Uncanny? Did the passengers of Flight 191 unconsciously, days before their deaths, have premonitions of disaster and send out messages for help? Did Booth pick up those messages?

Flight 191 has another story. According to Randles, film star Lindsay Wagner and her mother had been booked on Flight 191. Before boarding the plane,

Is it possible, through ESP, to "tune in" to future events?

Wagner was besieged by a horrible feeling about the flight; she decided to cancel and take a later one!

If Randles is right, then Booth and Wagner, and perhaps others, were being affected by a disturbance in the collective unconscious, which knew that a disaster would take place.

## Changing the Future?

Both proponents and opponents of ESP wonder, then, if the future is predetermined (that is, already set) or if it can be changed. Wagner seems to have been able to change her future—she survived. If the future *is* set, Wagner's survival might indicate that we are free to improvise within the boundaries of what

The tragic 1912 sinking of *The Titanic* was foreshadowed more than twenty years previously in Morgan Robertson's novel *The Wreck of the Titan.*

is already going to happen. We know that time and space affect us. We are born; we grow old. Our ability to move in the world is restricted. But can we, in turn, affect time and space?

Stephen King's novel *The Dead Zone* is based on exactly these speculations. The main character, psychic Johnny, comes into contact with a man trying to become president of the United States. Johnny, through psychic impressions, sees the man becoming president and starting World War III, a nuclear war. Because of his premonitions, Johnny intervenes and saves the world from potential destruction.

Is this just a fanciful story, or could it really happen? We'll probably never know. As Dr. J.B. Rhine pointed out, there's a problem with ESP accounts: "There's no way of coming to grips with them. They happen and are gone, leaving nothing but memory, none of the hard reality of a meteorite or a fossil."

Inquirers into ESP have wondered why ESP experiences are often related to disasters. Some theorizers think that ESP information may not break into conscious awareness unless it is very powerful, such as information that could save a person's life.

W.E. Cox, author of a study on railway accidents in the U.S., concluded that "fewer passengers [traveled by rail] on the day of the accident than on an average of 10 other days." Did passengers who normally would have ridden on accident days have unconscious premonitions of disaster and not travel as usual?

Martin Ebon, in *Prophecy of Our Time*, provides a possible clue:

There is a simple analogy about prophecy. If you are in a helicopter, circling over a mountain, and you can see two trains on opposite sides of the mountain heading toward each other—you can then foresee a collision as if you had superhuman knowledge. . . . Can we achieve a helicopter-like perception of our future?

Yes, certainly, to the degree to which each of us gains greater insight into himself—because we are

not so much masters as, unconsciously, magnets of our fate.

Ebon is saying that the more we grow as persons and the more we develop our inner abilities, such as the psychic ones, then the more we will be able to consciously direct our lives.

Author Zak Martin says this: "*Emotion* is the voltage of ESP." He adds that ESP works best when "accompanied by an emotional charge." Martin's statement could explain, too, why in early ESP experiments there was a decline effect: Subjects' scores went down the longer they were tested. They apparently lost their emotional zip and simply became bored.

Some critics say, however, that there was never any ESP to begin with. High scores were the result of luck or chance.

Since we're talking about human ESP, it might be interesting to explore whether animals have ESP.

Actress Lindsay Wagner had a premonition that she should not take Flight 191. Fortunately for her she changed flights. The plane she had been scheduled to travel on crashed, killing all on board. Directly above: Lindsay Wagner. Top: Flight 191, a tragedy foreseen in dreams by David Booth of Cincinnati.

Schoolteacher Richard Newton predicted in December 1979 that on March 15th, 1980 there would be a plane crash just outside a major population center in the northern hemisphere. The aircraft would have a red logo on its tail, and forty-five people would be killed. On March 17, 1980, a Royal Jordanian Airlines jet—with a red logo—crashed just outside Doha, in Qatar in the Persian Gulf, and forty-three people died. Did Newton use ESP to predict the crash? No; he did it all by statistics. He found by looking in aircraft books that more than half of the world's airlines have red somewhere in their logos. He knew that most of the world's flights are in the northern hemisphere, and that most crashes happen on take-off or landing. From a book called *Destination Disaster,* which listed all the world's air crashes, he discovered that March is the worst month of the year for crashes and that the second week in the month is the worst week. Finally, he found that the average number of fatalities in a crash is forty-five. So he used statistics to predict another crash, and he was almost exactly right. Above, he holds a chart graphing air crashes.

Can your dog or cat see the future? Consider this story told by writer George Laycock:

> Skippy's owner was a high school student, and he and his dog were exceptionally close companions. During the day, when the boy was at school, Skippy was lethargic and spent most of the time simply sleeping in the kitchen. This dog, too, could predict the boy's arrival accurately even though his time of returning varied. The dog always seemed to know that he was on his way and would run to the window, tail wagging wildly, to wait until the boy came into view.

> Both Skippy and his master were serious rabbit hunters, but one day the boy, accompanied by a friend, came home, picked up his shotgun, and noticed that Skippy reacted in an unusual manner. Normally, when the boy picked up his gun, the beagle, knowing that they were going hunting, began wagging its tail and leaping about happily. On this day, however, it looked up at its master, then turned slowly and went back into the house.

> The boy finally had to pick the dog up and carry it to the waiting car. Once in the field, the beagle's enthusiasm for hunting conquered its uneasiness. The hunt went normally enough until Skippy, running out of a patch of thick cover in front of his owner's friend, was mistaken for a rabbit. Skippy was shot by mistake and died from the gunshot wound. The owner then recalled that this was the first day ever that Skippy had not wanted to go hunting.

Author Martin Ebon likens prophecy (also called foresight or clairvoyance) to being in a helicopter where you can see over or through barriers that would ordinarily block the future from your sight.

## Animals and Seismographs

Animals also are reportedly able to predict earthquakes. According to Laycock, one scientist has said, "Dogs and cats belong to the class of finest animal seismographs. [A seismograph is a device that measures the severity and direction of earthquakes.] When an earthquake threatens, dogs either bark frantically, or howl or growl, and sometimes they whine pitifully."

Laycock states that in China people observe animals for any strange behavior that might indicate an earthquake is coming. He writes that in early February 1975, for example, Chinese farmers "began reporting that rats were coming out into the open and

Do our pets have ESP??

running around wildly. In addition, snakes were crawling out of the holes where they wintered and onto the ice. A medium-sized earthquake struck seventy miles away. . . . The animals were watched carefully. . . . Geese flew about wildly. Pigs tried to climb the walls to escape their pens. Horses and sheep were frantic.'' On February 4, 1975, a major earthquake hit the Haicheng province, but there were few casualties, as the warnings of the animals had caused people to move to safe areas.

Do animals really have psychic powers? Or do they simply have heightened senses? That is, are they more sensitive than people to subtle earth movements? No one knows for sure.

## More Animal ESP

There are other instances that may be evidence of animal ESP. It is said that birds will avoid landing on the branches of a tree about to be struck by lightning! How do they know? Zak Martin tells this story about birds:

> Just recently I noted a novel example of what appeared to be ESP among birds. Every day for several weeks I took the same London underground train,

Many people think that animals can sense when a natural disaster, such as an earthquake, is going to occur. Is this due to ESP—or simply to a strong awareness of natural signs like subtle earth movements?

58

Author Zak Martin believes that birds may have ESP, allowing them to anticipate danger before it occurs.

and every day the train 'rested' in a particular station, for five or ten minutes (the duration varied from day to day). As soon as the sliding doors opened, when the train came to a halt, in came the pigeons, scavenging on the crumbs of potato crisps dropped on the floor by passengers. Then, just seconds before the doors slid shut—and before the engine came to life— they hopped back out onto the platform.

I observed this ritual at least a dozen times, and never once did I see a pigeon trapped in the train when the doors closed.

Is there a connection between animal ESP and human ESP? It could be, Zak Martin suggests, that humans, more highly evolved than animals, forgot how to use ESP at some time in the past: "When we look down the evolutionary ladder, we can find increased evidence of psychic power. Even among members of our own species, it is those races of people that we regard as most primitive—i.e., less technologically advanced and less 'educated'—that are possessed of strong powers of ESP. The Australian aborigines, for instance, are renowned for their psychic feats."

Although there doesn't seem to be a clear-cut connection, it does seem that animals have what we could call an ESP sense. Who knows—perhaps our pets aren't only our best friends, but our best psychic friends!

"In 1956 the American psychic Jeane Dixon wrote in a magazine article: 'The 1960 election will be won by a Democrat, but he will be assassinated or die in office.'"

Author Stuart Holroyd, *Mysteries of the Mind*

"The death of a U.S. president while in office is not as improbable as it may seem. . . . Dixon's guess was later exploited, and with a few twists here and there the public was convinced she had named the date and place of the event."

Magician-columinst Henry Gordon, *Extra Sensory Deception*

Four

# Out-of-Body or Out-of-Mind?

I was very tired, physically exhausted, but my mind was rather active. I lay down on my bed to rest for a while in the late afternoon. I felt an odd prickly sensation in my limbs and then a buzzing sound. . . . I was conscious of some kind of pressure around or in my head and then I felt as if I was travelling along some dark tunnel, very fast. . . . This ended and I looked around me to find myself seemingly floating a few feet up in the air in my bedroom. I looked down and found my body underneath me. For some odd reason I was especially taken with an odd cobweb pattern on the top of my wardrobe. . . . I got a little scared by this and I willed myself to go back to my body. I got pulled back as if along some kind of cord or thread and it seemed to me, though I'm not certain, that I re-entered my body through my head. I gave a slight jump and sat up. It was completely unexpected. When I regained my wits I checked the wardrobe top. . . . the odd cobweb pattern was there all right!

This account, reported by Hans J. Eysenck and Carl Sargent in their book *Explaining the Unexplained,* is typical of what is known as an *Out-of-Body Experience,* or OBE. But, was this person really

out of his body? Was he dreaming? Or was he having an ESP experience?

## What Is an OBE?

No one seems to know exactly what happens during an OBE. Some people think that OBEs are ESP experiences. Remember remote viewing, the mind perceiving events or things from a distance? However the mind is able to do that, something similar could be happening with OBEs. In an OBE, however, an individual's mind feels as if it were completely outside the body, separate from it.

OBEs have been reported by people who have been in serious accidents or have suffered severe illnesses, perhaps nearly dying. They have suddenly and mysteriously found themselves hovering outside their bodies. Imagine your surprise if one day you fell asleep and found yourself looking down at your own sleeping face! You might not only be surprised—you might realize that although the body you're looking at is yours, you're not in your body!

Philosophers have always been interested in the relationship between the mind and body. No one has figured out whether a mind can exist without a body. If we can solve the mystery of OBEs, we might go a long way toward solving the age-old question of whether some part of us survives after death. If OBEs are a form of ESP, that information will be useful too. It would be just one more aspect of ESP that we might be able to develop and use.

## Near-Death Experiences

Interest in OBEs picked up in the 1970s as a result of the work done by two researchers, Dr. Elisabeth Kübler-Ross, a psychiatrist who works with dying patients, and Dr. Raymond A. Moody, author of the book *Life After Life*. Between the two of them, they amassed hundreds of accounts of "death" experiences in the form of OBEs.

Subjects interviewed by these researchers told of

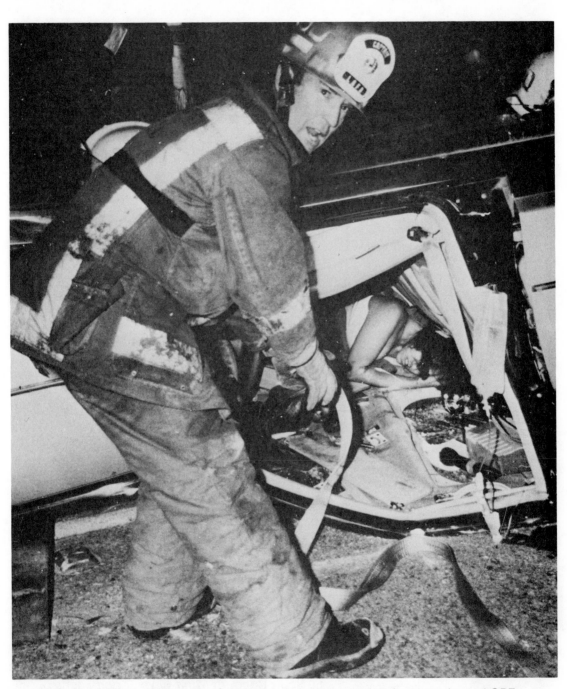

Many people who have been in serious accidents report that they experienced OBEs.

Elisabeth Kübler-Ross has done extensive research on the subject of death. Many patients she has worked with have described out-of-body experiences that were very similar to one another.

startling occurrences: They viewed their bodies from the outside! They usually felt as if they were near their beds, hovering above their bodies; they floated down a tunnel toward a light; they communicated with dead relatives; they telepathically received messages from higher beings; they saw the future; they saw distant locations; they felt wonderful and full of knowledge. Subjects also report being welcomed by someone at the ends of tunnels and of being asked to review their lives. Many report that their lives "flashed before their eyes." To those who experience them, OBEs feel vivid, real, and clear.

One of Moody's subjects described leaving his body after a heart attack: "It was dark—you could call it a hole or a tunnel—and there was this bright light. It got brighter and brighter. And I seemed to go *through* it. All of a sudden I was just somewhere else. There was a gold-looking light, everywhere. Beautiful. I couldn't find a source anywhere. It was just all around, coming from everywhere."

D. Scott Rogo, in *Mind Beyond Body*, tells of one

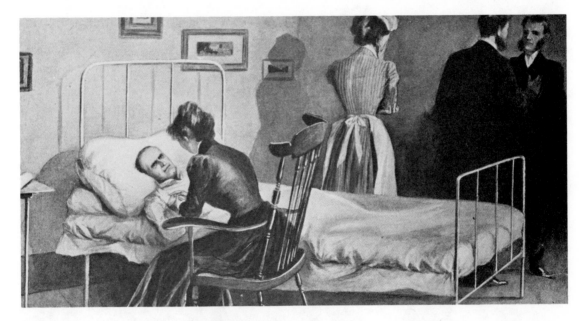

of his own experiences: "I began to feel oddly chilly and started to tremble. I flipped over onto my side, realizing at the same moment that my whole body was pulsating [vibrating] and that I was almost paralyzed. . . . An instant later I found myself floating in the air and, in another instant, I was standing at the foot of the bed staring at myself. I made an attempt to [turn] about-face . . . and tried to walk toward the door to my room, which led to a hallway. I felt as though I were gliding through jelly as I moved, and I lost balance for a moment and almost fell over. Everything was blurred by a cloudy hue that enveloped a whitish form, which I perceived as my body. A moment later I found myself awakening in my bed. But I also realized that I had never been asleep."

Writer Susan Blackmore describes an incident involving a woman in an L-shaped hospital ward who couldn't see around the corner to the other beds in the room:

One morning I felt myself floating upwards, and

Many dying people report bright lights, feelings of well-being, and visions of higher beings. Do these signify that there is life after death, or are they merely hallucinations?

D. Scott Rogo, author of many books on ESP and related phenomena, has had his own OBEs.

found I was looking down on the rest of the patients. I could see myself propped up against pillows, very white and ill. I saw the sister and nurse rush to my bed with oxygen. Then everything went blank. The next I remember was opening my eyes to see the sister bending over me.

I told her what had happened, but at first she thought I was rambling. Then I said, "There is a big woman sitting up in bed with her head wrapped in bandages; and she is knitting something with blue wool. She has a very red face!" This certainly shook her [the nurse], as apparently the lady concerned had a mastoid [neck] operation and was just as I described.

Novelist Ernest Hemingway was nineteen when he served at the Italian Front in World War I. After being wounded by a mortar shell, he said, "I felt my soul or something coming right out of my body, like you'd pluck a silk handkerchief out of a pocket by one corner. It flew around and then came back and went in again, and I wasn't dead anymore."

## OBEs and Reality

In an OBE study performed by parapsychologist Celia Green, several subjects made these statements about their experiences:

- "Reality was my 'floating self' and the objects below seemed as shadows against the reality of my floating self."
- "I have never been so wide awake or experienced such a wonderful sense of freedom before."
- "I had no further interest in my physical body, or indeed my physical life. I only wanted to pursue

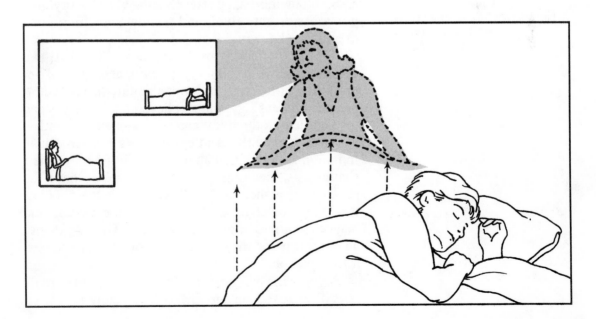

An artist's version of one hospital patient's out-of-body experience.

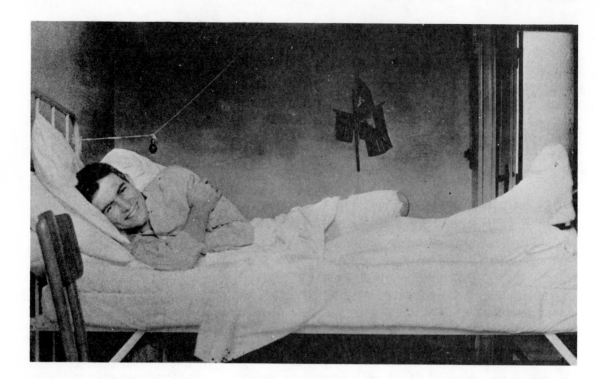

The young Ernest Hemingway experienced an OBE when he was badly injured in World War I.

and prolong this happy state of being where everything was more bright, vivid, and real than anything I had previously known.''

Such experiences are hardly new. The OBE is a common theme in folklore, religion, and cultural anthropology (the study of human cultures). For example, the ancient Egyptians believed that during sleep the soul leaves the body and comes back; at death it leaves permanently. And certain Eskimo, American Indian, and Australian aboriginal tribes believe their shamans—''medicine people'' or priests—have the power to leave their bodies. When outside their bodies, they may travel to another part of the world, and maybe even into another dimension. They do this to gain information they may need—for example, to heal a sick person.

What's the explanation for OBEs? Are they real? Is ESP involved, or are OBEs completely unrelated to ESP?

Author Jenny Randles thinks OBEs could be ESP experiences. She believes they may happen when the mind switches to an extrasensory way of experiencing life. Furthermore, she believes OBEs are probably purely subjective—that is, they happen only in the mind; the person experiencing them doesn't *actually* leave the body.

Another interpretation of this phenomenon is what some people have long called "astral projection." Astral projection is based on the belief that everyone has an inner, finer body that can be sent outside the

Many people believe their priests can leave the body to go on spiritual quests.

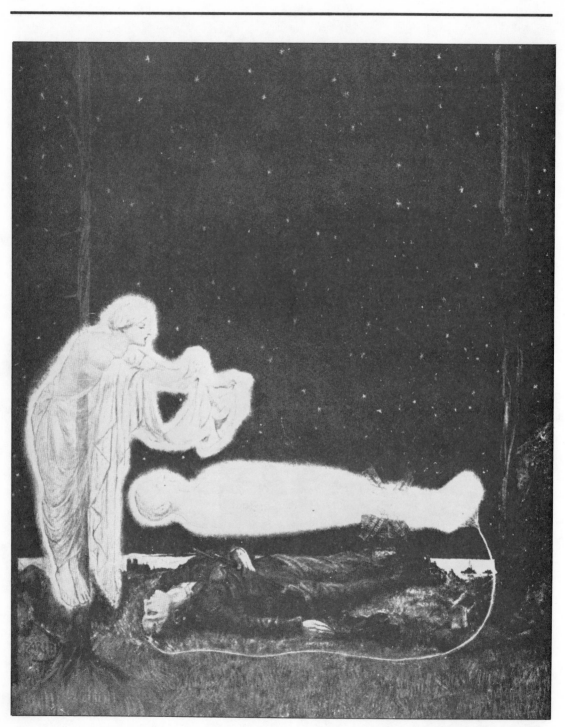

This painting depicts the "inner body" connected to the physical body by a "psychic umbilical cord."

physical body. Many people who have had OBEs, however, report that, when out of the body, they only experience themselves as a formless mind or consciousness, not as a body.

## Science and OBEs

What has science done to investigate OBEs? Basically, it has attempted to answer three major questions: One, can anything be detected that leaves the body? Two, if people have OBEs, can they travel to distant locations, gather information, and bring it back? Three, what is the biological state during an OBE?

In regard to the first question, writer Susan Blackmore says, "Generally physical detectors have performed the worst [in regard to detection]. Magnetometers, ultra-violet and infra-red detectors, strain gauges, thermistors, and detectors of magnetic and electrical effects have all been used, but there has rarely been a response at all. . . . At the moment it appears that no reliable physical detection system has been found." Blackmore concludes, "All these results seem to imply either that nothing does leave the body in an OBE, or that whatever does leave is remarkably hard to detect."

If perception of distant locations is possible during an OBE, this suggests that ESP might be going on. In typical experiments, subjects have been asked to induce an OBE and travel to a place where there are pre-arranged objects. Subjects were asked to describe what they saw. Blackmore reports that those experiments have been inconclusive. The problem of studying OBEs is the same as in regular ESP experiments: Is it possible to consciously cause OBEs, or is performance really measurable only when spontaneous OBEs occur?

With these two types of investigations turning up poor results, the reality of OBEs might seem questionable. Yet Blackmore reports that findings about

"Near-death experiences and deathbed visions are nothing but hallucinations triggered by the enormously stressful situation near death."

Psychologist Ronald K. Siegel, *American Psychologist*

"Calling such experiences hallucinations or delusions may solve the problem for Siegel, but . . . naming experiences in this manner does not seem to lead one any nearer the truth of the experience. His data and conclusions seem sparse."

Parapsychologist Janet Lee Mitchell, *Out-of-Body Experiences*

Parapsychologist Susan Blackmore has done much research on OBEs and other psychic phenomena. Here she is testing her own baby Emily for psychic power. She hoped to determine whether the baby could affect a computer program with her mind.

OBE physiology (state of the body's functioning) are more encouraging:

Subjects have been asked to induce OBEs. During the OBE, their heart rates, eye movements, and brain waves were monitored. The results of these experiments, Blackmore says, show that OBEs don't occur during the state associated with dreaming. This would seem to indicate, then, that OBEs are not just dreams—one of the explanations given to account for them.

Moreover, subjects say that during an OBE they're wide awake and thinking. We know from common experience what it's like to be awake and thinking. Also, each state of mind—waking, dreaming, sleeping—has its own characteristic physiological state. In each state, bodily and mental activity is different. By monitoring these states in persons having an OBE, it should be possible to discover when OBEs take place. If they don't happen in the dream state, as Blackmore contends, then they can't be simply be identified with dreams.

John Palmer, however, in an issue of *Parapsychology Review*, says that he thinks OBEs *are* a part of sleep; specifically, *hypnogogic* sleep, a state of being half-awake and half-asleep, in which the mind experiences dreamlike images, colors, lights, vivid images of faces, of strangers, and of landscapes. Palmer believes that hypnogogic sleep accounts for the majority of OBEs, and that an OBE is "neither potentially nor actually a psychic phenomenon. It is an experience or mental state, like a dream or any other altered state of consciousness." He explains the phenomenon as "ego-splitting: As well as feeling unnaturally calm, the subject . . . feels as though he is actually *outside himself.*"

Many physicians agree with Palmer that OBEs are hallucinations (seeing imaginary things that seem real). They contend that OBEs could be brought on by a condition where the brain is starved of oxygen.

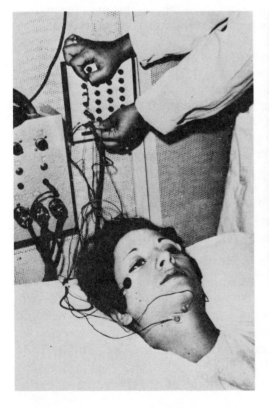

Left: A young woman is hooked up to special equipment in a dream telepathy experiment. Some scientists believe that OBEs are really a form of sleep. Right: Professor Charles Tart adjusts a special measuring instrument used in studies of out-of-body experiences.

"Many people of excellent reputation and critical intelligence have not only reported out-of-body experiences but have also tested them sufficiently to become convinced that they have actually traveled away from where their bodies were."

Parapsychologist Janet Lee Mitchell, *Out-of-Body Experiences*

"The laboratory work on OBEs seemed largely unconvincing. . . . Most of the results were much like those of any other ESP experiments. That is, the effects were always small and often inconsistent."

Parapsychologist Susan Blackmore, in *A Skeptic's Handbook of Parapsychology*

But how could this explain seeing *oneself* during an OBE? James E. Alcock, in *Paranormal Borderlines of Science*, remarks that some people "argue that hallucinations of one's own image are very rare in hypnogogic sleep," but he reports that two researchers discovered that some subjects do see themselves.

Kenneth King, author of *Heading Toward Omega*, describes the experience of a man named Tom Sawyer, who was pinned beneath a truck. Sawyer tells of moving through a tunnel during an OBE:

All this time, the speed is increasing. . . . Gradually you realize . . . you're going at least the speed of light.

And then you gradually realize that *way*, way off in the distance—again, unmeasurable distance—it appears that it might be the end of the tunnel. And all you see is a white light. . . .

And then before you is this—is this most magnificent, just gorgeous, beautiful, bright, white or blue-white light.

The next sensation is this wonderful, wonderful feeling of this light. . . . Then the light immediately communicates to you. . . . This communication is what you might call telepathic. It's absolutely instant, absolutely clear. . . .

The second most magnificent experience . . . is when you realize that you are suddenly in communication with absolute, total knowledge. . . . You can think of a question . . . and immediately know the answer to it.

Hallucination? It sounds like either an OBE or ESP experience. Or maybe both mixed together.

## Visions of the Future

Kenneth King discovered that OBE subjects tend to experience visions of the future, either on a personal or a global level. Interestingly enough, King finds that while there is variety in the personal visions, the global visions all seem to be similar. They all seem to deal with global disasters that are supposed to happen toward the end of this century: earth-

Most people who have experienced OBEs describe the feeling of traveling through a tunnel.

Dr. Jan Ehrenwald believes that OBEs reflect the human desire for immortality.

Baseball player Gary Gaetti made the final out in the 1987 World Series. He said, "It was like in a dream. I wasn't even there; I was the left field camera. I wasn't in my body at all. . . . It was definitely an out-of-body experience."

quakes, shifts in the earth's structure, and economic collapse on a worldwide scale. Following the disasters will be world peace.

One subject had an OBE and vision in 1967: "The vision of the future I received during my near-death experience was one of tremendous upheaval in the world."

Some critics, though, think that these experiences are not at all mysterious; they are psychological in origin, involving memory, imagination, illnesses of the mind, and fear of death. Are OBEs projections of one's own fear of the future or of one's own unconscious problems? Does an individual near death change his or her own death into a vision of earth-shaking importance?

Kenneth King doesn't think so. The strong similarity of so many of the global visions seems like more than coincidence to him. King also believes that mental illness can be disregarded as the source of OBEs. Why? First, he says, there's no reason to assume that *all* such experiences are caused by mental illness; second, he believes a mental problem most likely would be the *result* of a vision, not its source; third, he asks, even if future events are seen by truly disturbed people, couldn't they still be real? What do you think—is King right?

## OBEs: Coping with Death?

Criticism that OBEs are no more than ways our minds try to cope with the idea of death may or may not hold up.

Jan Ehrenwald says this: "OBEs are expressions of man's perennial quest for immortality, they are faltering attempts to assert the reality and autonomous [self-governing] existence of the 'soul'—a deliberate challenge to the threat of extinction." Humans don't want to die, so perhaps we imagine ways out of truly dying—one of them being OBEs, where our mind or soul survives.

D. Scott Rogo explains his view of the dispute: "Just because the OBE may be a method of defying death does not mean that it is a purely symbolic and/or hallucinatory experience. The fact that man has a psychological need to believe in an afterlife does not automatically mean that we do not survive death."

Is an OBE a denial of death? A World War II medic who "died" in a plane crash wrote this: "One interesting effect this experience had upon me was the great removal of any fear of death, because of the extraordinarily pleasant experience of what one felt and became aware of when one was apparently detached from one's body." Such testimony would appear to contradict the denial-of-death theory.

The questions still remain unanswered: Are OBEs psychic phenomena? Are they imaginary? Do mind and body use two separate energies? Can we truly leave our bodies? Until someone comes up with definite answers, these questions will remain.

"Once the OBE has begun . . . the person may feel that he possesses a 'charged' wakefulness—details often seem clear and impress the observer as real, not dreamlike or fantastic."

Author Bernard Gittelson, *Intangible Evidence*

"The fact that people are generally unable to describe target materials when they claim to be 'astrally' located at a site is strong evidence in favor of a hallucination-fantasy explanation of OBEs."

Former parapsychological researcher Douglas Stokes, in *A Skeptic's Handbook of Parapsychology*

Five

# Psychokinesis: May the Force Be with You

H ave you ever tried to make someone who was ill better through the power of your thoughts? Have you tried to influence dice or playing cards? Do you believe you could bend a spoon or slide objects across a table with just your mind? Do you think your thoughts alone can affect the world in some way? Consider what happened with D. Scott Rogo:

> Some years ago I discovered that a very good friend of mine had acted quite dishonorably toward me, which angered me to no end. He had just bought a Mercedes-Benz which was, of course, his pride and joy. I was miles away in a different city at the time and, very childishly, I couldn't keep from thinking how I would like to wreck the car in order to get even. When I arrived back home only a few days later, I learned that, at the very time of my mental vendetta [act of revenge], the car had been completely destroyed in a freak accident. I was unnerved, for I could not help but feel that somehow my thoughts had helped precipitate the accident.

Is it possible that our thoughts can cause accidents? Is it possible that our minds can affect physical things? If so, how responsible are we for things that happen just as we wish them to? For example, was Rogo

Is it possible that our thoughts can cause accidents?

responsible for his friend's car wreck? If it is possible to affect physical matter, can we then affect other people's lives? These are not far-fetched questions, and someday we may know all the answers. But answers to some of them may already be yes, according to evidence gathered on an ESP-related phenomenon, *psychokinesis,* or PK for short. Psychokinesis means "mind movement" or "mind over matter." It is the ability to affect objects—that is, to make them move or change—by the sheer force of the mind.

## Mind Affecting Matter

Throughout this book, we have seen ESP described as a mental phenomenon involving mind and objects. PK, on the other hand, seems to be a *physical* phenomenon involving mind and objects. In most forms of ESP, the mind *receives* incoming impressions and information about events, objects, and people; in

PK, the mind *projects outward* to influence objects or events. For example, Rogo sent out a mental order for his friend's car to be demolished.

Researchers suggest that if we can solve the mystery of either ESP or PK, we'll solve the mystery of both because each involves interaction between mind and objects. Thus, both PK and ESP could be operating off the same energy or principle. Researchers ask, what is the link between mind and matter? This is a question that has been asked since the days of the Greek philosophers, and no one has figured it out. If we simply dismiss as ridiculous the idea of mind having control over matter, we might ask ourselves, as scientist and writer Arthur C. Clarke asks, ''What happens when we decide to move our little finger?'' Although Clarke suggests that a link between mind and matter does exist, he can't solve the problem: What exactly connects the mind to the body? What do you think?

The relationship between PK and ESP is important because ESP may not really be ESP; it may really be PK. John Fairley and Simon Welfare, the authors

We know that the brain controls the movements of our body. Can it also control the movements of other things?

Why are some people unusually lucky at guessing the winners of events like horseraces? Might they be affecting the outcome with their PK energy?

of *Arthur C. Clarke's World of Strange Powers*, write: "Some researchers believe that most paranormal phenomena can be explained in terms of PK; someone who 'foresees' a winner in a horserace might really be using PK to make the horse win; firewalkers [people who walk barefooted over burning coals] might be able to cool the brands [coals] beneath their feet; and poltergeists [mischievous noisy ghosts] . . . might be just PK in action."

Yet others believe that ESP and PK are separate powers which might be coming from the same energy. Is there an answer to the mystery? Let's look at some background on PK.

**Dice Tests**

PK tests began at Duke University in the 1930s with Dr. J.B. Rhine. Rhine had met a gambler who claimed that gamblers often used their minds to influence the fall of dice and playing cards. Intrigued by this notion, Rhine set up experiments using dice to test PK. According to D. Scott Rogo, in *Minds and Motion*, "Subjects threw dice . . . trying to make selected die [singular form of 'dice'] faces come up more often than any others; or for doubles to result more often than chance would account for; or to make the dice land on certain positions of a landing platform. All these tests were ultimately successful.'' The results showed that something more than chance was involved. They seemed to prove that ''the mind could really exert a psychical force onto the physical world.''

Rogo further reports that the tests established a substantial connection between PK and ESP: ''The mind had to keep track of the rolling and bouncing dice as they fell so it could make them land in the required position.'' Rogo says that it was ESP that was responsible for organizing the incoming information about the dice. His implication is that ESP and PK are like two sides of a coin. On one side, ESP is needed to take in information about objects such as dice, so that, on the other side, PK can occur. Rogo concludes that both function together. He cites tests performed in Great Britain that seem to confirm his conclusion: ''For these tests, subjects had to roll dice to make them land (the PK task) on sides which would match a list of numbers in sealed envelopes (which they had to determine by ESP). Again, the results were positive.''

Rhine's early tests, however, have been criticized for not being well designed or properly executed, and especially because of the inability of other ex-

Below: Dr. J.B. Rhine was the first to seriously attempt to study psychic phenomena in a systematic and scientific way. Below left: One of Rhine's PK dice experiments done during the 1930s.

84

"PK is a force of incredible magnitude and longevity."

Parapsychologist D. Scott Rogo,
*Minds and Motion*

"There is a general feeling among the public that some of these [PK] phenomena exist—but the truth is that there has never been any strong evidence to prove it."

Magician-columnist Henry Gordon,
*Extra Sensory Deception*

perimenters to reproduce Rhine's results. For instance, in Rhine's early tests, subjects threw the dice with their hands. Hand-throwing leaves open the possibility of cheating as well as that of unconscious influence on the way the dice fall. (Later, machines were devised that would eliminate human influence.) Also, on many occasions, subjects tested themselves without witnesses present to confirm results. According to Arthur Clarke, one British skeptic (doubter) said, "The Duke experimenters seem to have fallen into pitfalls that the intelligent schoolboy should have avoided."

### Temperature Test

The PK phenomenon isn't limited to the rolling of dice. Cases have been reported of people being able to move furniture and to break or bend metal objects such as spoons and knives. There are also reports of people being able to control the temperature of a room or an object.

One experiment was conducted by Dr. Gertrude Schmeidler at the City College of City University of New York. She set up a test to investigate claims made by psychic Ingo Swann that he could change the surface temperature of an object while sitting at a distance from it. She arranged a group of thermos bottles at different distances from Swann. Each thermos had a piece of graphite inside and an electrode wire connected to a polygraph machine that would record temperature changes. In each test, Dr. Schmeidler chose a target thermos and told Swann to raise or lower the temperature of the graphite inside. Amazingly, in seven out of ten series of tests, the polygraph showed that the temperature of the target item rose or lowered significantly as Swann willed it to. Swann did what he said he could do.

### Stopping Clocks

Another common PK phenomenon reported from around the world is that of clocks stopping when someone dies. Rogo cites an instance of a man whose

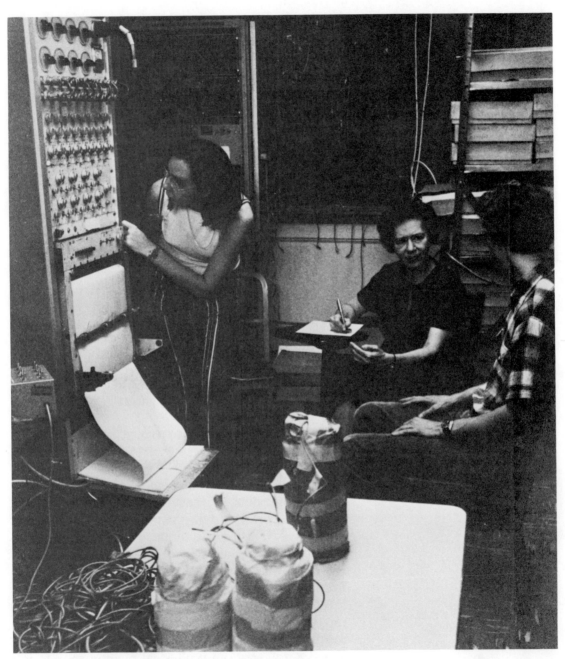

Dr. Gertrude Schmeidler and the equipment used to test mental control over temperature.

brother had once given him a gold watch:

I took leave from my job and sat up nights to help my sister-in-law during the last two days of my brother's terminal illness. He breathed his last at six-twenty-five in the morning. I called the family immediately and we phoned for the doctor and the undertakers. At about seven-thirty we were sitting around a rush breakfast. . . . As the wall clock neared nine o'clock, I suggested it was time the widow and my brothers made arrangements to get started for the funeral parlor. Someone asked me how much time we had, and I took [out] the pocket watch mentioned above, when, lo and behold, it had stopped at the exact moment of his death.

Rogo relates another incident, quoting a woman named Camille Flammarian as she told the story to her son:

One night . . . in our bedroom, we were awakened by a great noise; we had heard a mirror on the mantelpiece fall down, as well as your father's watch-stand. I got up, and found that the mirror had fallen upon the hearth; the watch had been thrown upon the floor on one side and the watchstand on the other. . . . In the morning when I got up, we found that nothing had been broken.

The same morning the postman brought us a letter telling us of the death of your Aunt Boyet, your father's sister, who had died that very night.

How are such experiences explained? Are they merely coincidences? Early PK investigators believed that some part of a dying person's mind would visit a relative's house and announce his or her death by producing a physical occurrence, such as a mirror falling off a wall or a clock stopping. But Dr. Louisa Rhine believed that such coincidences are actually created by the witnesses, not the deceased. Rogo reports, "Her theory is that the witness unconsciously receives an ESP impression of the death and then projects PK to carry out a physical phenomenon to jolt the message into consciousness." In other words, PK

Dr. Louisa Rhine

could be a result of ESP.

In November 1973, on a television talk show in Great Britain, Israeli psychic Uri Geller apparently demonstrated an ability to bend metal objects— psychically. Moreover, viewers reported that inside their homes strange things happened: Broken watches started running again, and keys and knives bent for no reason. Thereafter, Geller became one of the most controversial figures in the history of psychic phenomena, both for his ESP and his PK claims. Rogo tells a typical story about Geller's feats:

> One of these incidents was reported by Gerald Feinberg, a Columbia University physicist, and one of America's most esteemed scientists. Feinberg was having lunch with Geller [and others] . . . when Geller suddenly decided to give one of his spontaneous demonstrations. He spontaneously asked [former Apollo astronaut Edgar] Mitchell's secretary to take off her gold ring and clench it in her fist. He

waved his hand over hers and then asked her to open her fist.

"She opened it up," recalls Feinberg, "and the ring then appeared with a crack in it, as if it had been cut with a very sharp instrument. . . . But even more interesting, he took the ring and put it down on a table where several of us were sitting. Over a period of a couple of hours, the ring twisted. . . . It twisted so that it went gradually into the shape of an 'S.' "

Rogo reports another incident that happened when Geller was dining with Mitchell:

The incident occurred during a lunch break at the Stanford Research Institute [SRI] cafeteria. Geller was undergoing a series of tests at SRI at the time and was lunching with Mitchell and SRI physicist Harold Puthoff. [Geller] was eating his ice cream dessert when his spoon struck something hard. "We cleaned the ice cream off the metal," declared Geller, "and saw that it's a piece of a broken tie clasp."

Mitchell took the broken tie clasp from Geller and casually examined it. But his nonchalant attitude

Israeli psychic Uri Geller is known for his ability to use mental energy to perform physical feats. Here, he is shown bending a spoon merely by concentrating and lightly rubbing it.

soon transformed into wild enthusiasm. "My God," exclaimed the startled astronaut, who continued after composing himself, "Well, about three years ago I got a present from Bear Archery Company. . . . they gave me a pin exactly like you have in your ice cream."

## A Magician Disagrees

Another mysterious power? Could Geller make objects appear out of thin air? Stage magician James Randi would definitely say no. Since the 1960s, Randi has campaigned against "the profit- and publicity-seeking ESP psychic crowd." Also, Randi has offered $10,000 to "anyone who can perform a single demonstration of a paranormal, supernatural, or occult [mysterious] nature, under properly observed conditions." No one has yet walked away with the money. Randi has stated that he is convinced that Geller is a clever magician, nothing more.

If so, then how does Geller succeed in his demonstrations? Simple, according to Randi: Geller

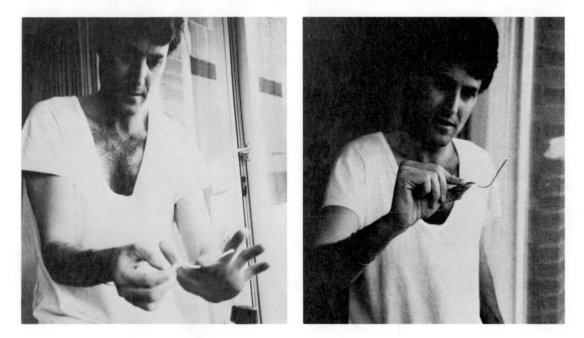

Above left: Professional magician and psychic investigator James Randi thinks that Uri Geller is a fraud. Randi has never found a supposed psychic event that he has not believed has had a reasonable explanation. Above right: Former astronaut Edgar Mitchell witnessed Uri Geller's remarkable PK feats and found them convincing.

uses tricks that involve sleight-of-hand; he distracts an audience's attention, receives signals from partners, and switches objects.

Does Geller really use PK to bend spoons? Again, no, if Randi is right. Geller, through sleight-of-hand movements, can replace the original spoon with one already pre-stressed or conditioned to break with little effort, states Randi. By distracting an audience's attention, Geller can bend an object while no one is looking.

But what would explain this account by one writer: "He [Geller] told us to get out our keys. . . . With thumb and forefinger, Geller rubbed lightly the top of a heavy metal key we had supplied. After about a minute he said, 'Look, look! It's doing it. It's bending.' And so it was. We placed it on the desk and as we talked it continued to bend. No one touched it.'' Randi might be right about substitutions, but what about a key that keeps bending?

## Paranormal or Normal?

Some of Randi's exposés of ESP frauds aren't without a comic side. Authors John Fairley and Simon Welfare report that Randi once had an assistant "Pose [as a psychic] on a radio show and asked listeners to ring in with reports of any strange manifestations [physical occurrences] that occurred during the broadcast. The calls that began to flood the switchboard showed that the assistant's non-existent 'powers' were every bit as dramatic as Geller's: Mirrors cracked, cats ran amok [wildly], a light bulb exploded, cracks appeared in a window, an air-conditioner and a refrigerator stopped working, toilet paper fell off the roll.'' The point is, all these were things that might normally happen regardless of whether a real or a fake psychic was on a radio show.

Authors Hans J. Eysenck and Carl Sargent, in *Explaining the Unexplained*, tell of research on PK that

Is it possible to bend silverware, break keys, and pull lost tie clasps out of thin air by using PK?

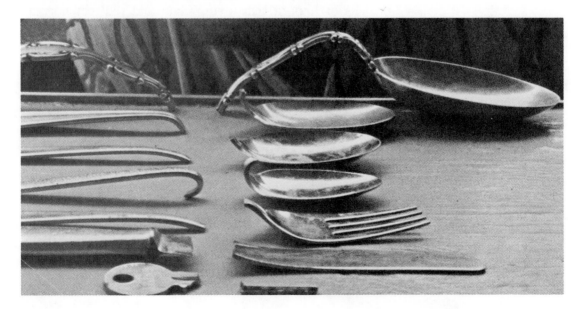

appears favorable. The most startling research involved a Frenchman named Jean-Paul Girard. According to the authors, "Crussard and Bouvaist [researchers] have been able to record the bending of metal strips in *completely sealed* glass tubes with the French metal-bender Jean-Paul Girard," and "have been able to obtain bending of metal rods [by Girard] which would require a force in excess of [human] physical strength." Thus, even if Girard had physically tried to bend the rods, which he didn't—he used his mind—he wouldn't have succeeded because the rods were too strong for a man to bend. The authors conclude: "Such evidence as this cannot be dismissed easily. . . . We are no longer in Gellerland."

## Theories

What then is PK? Rogo suggests that there are three possibilities: "The first type might be some sort of energy, let's call it psi [psychic] energy, as Rhine does, which is ignited by a conscious or unconscious act of will. This psi energy could take two guises [appearances]. It may either generate power to achieve its end, or it may manipulate and redirect normal sources of energy." In short, Rogo suggests that ESP may result from non-physical, psychic energy rather than physical energy. He has no idea, however, exactly what this energy could be.

"The second type of PK power we possess may be some sort of biological plasma [a kind of mysterious fluid or gas] which is capable of exteriorizing from [leaving] the body. This force could be linked to psi energy." This second suggestion is probably the least likely. A fluid would be physical; hence, we should be able to detect it.

"Third, I can't dismiss the possibility that man might also have the ability to channel some sort of cosmic force or life-force as well. This force might pervade [spread throughout] the universe and, on certain occasions, we might act as batteries or generators

Schoolchildren used their mental energy to make this "scrunch" of paperclips inside a glass ball. They experimented with their PK powers in Professor John B. Hasted's laboratory at the University of London.

for it.'' Rogo's third possibility describes what might be a universal energy, something like gravity. Since it would be everywhere, it could be tapped into anywhere.

Loyd Auerbach also comments about PK and says that it:

> raises questions about the kind of influence that may be going on, or what kind of energy is involved, or even the level on which the influence is occurring. For example, how can a mind reach out and invisibly and without detection, move an object across a table or affect the inner workings of a computer? When a piece of metal is bent, is the mind of the PK agent [person doing PK] reaching out with an invisible-force "hand" to bend the metal, or does the mind go down into the structure of that metal and rearrange the configuration of the metal's molecules so as to change it to a bent form? Or is the space in which the metal piece exists being changed, so that the metal bends with it?

Good questions. Rogo, at least, doesn't believe

A man levitates in this picture from 17th-century England. The mysteries of ESP have been of interest to people for as long as we have human records.

anyone will solve the mystery soon. As PK writer Diana Robinson has said, "It is a long step from deciding whether dice can be influenced by the mind to deciding that perhaps, if you get your head straight, the universe will automatically tend to fulfill your needs. It is a long step, but, if it is true, it is probably the most important step anyone can take."

"In the last analysis, the only resolution of the impasse between parapsychologists and their critics will come from the *evidence* itself."

Philosophy professor Paul Kurtz, "Is Parapsychology a Science?"

"To rely exclusively on the experimental evidence to settle the question of the basic existence of psi is to betray a profound misunderstanding of the role of experimentation in science."

Psychology professor John Beloff, "What Is Your Counter-Explanation? A Plea to Skeptics To Think Again"

# Six

# ESP and You

B y now you may be asking, is everyone psychic, and, can ESP be developed? According to writer Loyd Auerbach, everyone does have psychic abilities, "but the frequency and strength of psi experiences vary quite a bit, and appear to depend on many factors." For example, some people have more control over their ESP than others. They can consciously create a state of mind where ESP can happen. For most people, ESP could be happening constantly, yet they aren't aware of it. Auerbach says that having ESP experiences "is a normal thing. . . . If we get reported experiences from people of all ages, nationalities, cultures, religions, and physical conditions, then to have a psychic experience is to be within that range of human behavior we call 'normal.' Not 'crazy' or 'weird' or 'bizarre,' merely normal."

If ESP is probably happening all the time, how is it that we're not conscious of it? Auerbach explains that it has to do with what psychologists call "the cocktail party effect": Your ears can pick up a range of sounds over a certain range of distance. So what happens when you are engaged in a conversation in a crowded room, and you suddenly get bored . . . ?

A fifteen-year-old girl attempts to "read" a notebook through a thick blindfold. Is it possible for us to learn to use ESP?

You tune out that conversation and zero in on sounds or conversations somewhere else in the room . . . your ears could obviously pick up every conversation in the room, perhaps shifting attention from one to another. . . . Think of psi in the same way, always operating, but needing your attention."

Further, Auerbach says to consider your ESP this way: It "scans the environment for information, objects, and events that could help fill a need you have, whether you are consciously or unconsciously aware of that need."

## Developing ESP

Can anyone develop ESP? ESP supporters say that although everyone has the potential for ESP, that potential needs to be developed. It's like anything else in life we want to be good at whether it be basketball, computer programming, or painting: It takes practice. Unfortunately, there's no sure-fire way to do this. There are classes that one can take, but, as Auerbach remarks, "It seems that any one psychic development course may help a few people, but no technique seems to be universal. In fact, it may be that the technique taught only works for the person teaching it."

In other words, some people may have stumbled across their own ESP, but the way in which they did it may not work for others. All anyone can do is experiment with techniques offered in books or classes and see what happens. Zak Martin writes, "There is a universe of untapped power, an infinite resource within the psychic reach of every person . . . just waiting to be discovered and explored." Hence, if we can locate and tap into that resource, our ESP abilities will grow.

Martin reports one story from a woman who found her psychic abilities while pretending to be "Madame Za Za" at a party:

I was all dressed, gypsy style, with a sequinned headscarf and huge circular earrings. My first

A party fortune-teller discovered she had real ESP powers.

customer was a young woman who was, I later found out, a teacher at the school. I took both her hands and pretended to scrutinize [study] them closely, as I imagined a real palmist [palm reader] would. In fact, I knew nothing at all about palmistry, and I was desperately trying to think of something to say—but my mind was a complete blank, despite the fact that I had rehearsed my "spiel" [salespitch] all week.

Finally, after several long minutes of mutual embarrassment during which I must have said "Hmm, that's interesting" at least a dozen times, I suddenly heard myself saying "You are married to a man who is a foreigner, and you are having a secret affair with an older man whose initial is M."

Even as I spoke, I wanted to bite my tongue. To my great surprise, however, the young woman turned pale and admitted at once that what I said was correct.

Although the woman was simply play-acting as a psychic, in the crisis of the moment her ESP abilities announced themselves!

A person with developed ESP skills could put them to many good uses. Healing and archaeology are only two of the numerous possibilities.

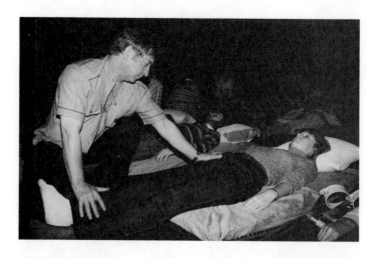

Imagine this: You have ESP. Then what? What can you do with it? Is it an ability you could use in a practical way, or just something you could show off with? Loyd Auerbach points out that ESP can be used in a number of ways to benefit yourself and others. For one thing, you might be able to prevent tragedies such as plane and car accidents if you saw them coming. You might be able to locate oil, gas, and water in the ground or missing persons and objects.

Another interesting possibility for using ESP is in archaeology. Archaeology is the study of past human civilizations through relics found or dug up in the ground. Some psychics seem to be able to point out the best spots to dig. As a psychic, you might also be able to hold a relic—for example, a pot or vase or tool—and through ESP, perceive information about the person who made the object.

Another way to use ESP would be preventing or solving crimes. Police departments throughout the world have used psychics on mysterious cases. Sometimes the psychics have given important information about the crime.

Another area in which ESP could be used is psychic healing. This is healing sickness or injury in a way that is unexplainable from a medical standpoint.

Some psychic healers claim to have cured an illness or healed a wound in an unusually fast time; some claim to have completely reversed a critical physical condition such as cancer. Psychic healers are reported to be working not only in the U.S., but also in the Philippines and in South America.

Finally, it is conceivable that you could use ESP to improve your finances. For example, maybe someday you'll want to own your own business but won't know if you should or shouldn't go ahead with it. ESP could help you make the right decision by informing you about the possible success or failure of your business.

These are just a few ideas on how to put ESP to use. Any ideas of your own?

## Conclusion

# The Search Goes On. . . .

This book could only scratch the surface of the mysteries of ESP. It seems that when we ask questions about ESP, we raise more questions: Do people differ in their ESP abilities? What conditions are best for ESP? Will science ever be able to explain ESP, or is it beyond the laws of science? None of these questions has ready answers.

What are we to make of all this? Perhaps all anyone can do is to keep an open mind and continue to explore the mysteries of ESP.

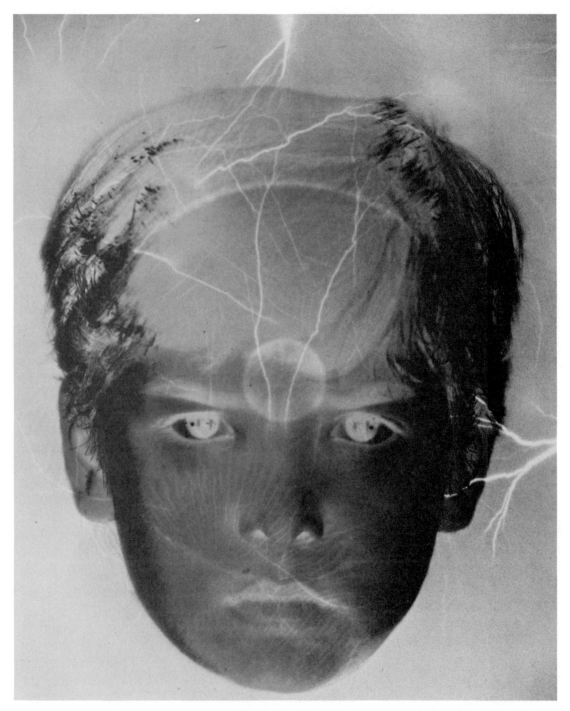

Will we ever be able to absolutely prove that ESP exists? Will we ever be able to explain its mysteries?

# Appendix

# ESP Tests for Fun

C urious to see if you have ESP? Here are some easy experiments to try.

**Telepathy**

Take twenty-five blank index cards and draw one of the following symbols on each card: a cross, a square, a circle, a star, and wavy lines. Each symbol should be on five cards. Now you have your own Zener deck.

Shuffle the cards. Have a friend hold the cards and concentrate on mentally sending the symbols to you, one at a time.

As you indicate which symbol you believe is being sent, your friend should write down each try as a hit or a miss. Repeat the experiment until you have completed a hundred tries—that's how J.B. Rhine did it, remember? If you hit more than twenty out of a hundred cards, chances are your guesses aren't mere coincidence.

Let your friend try the experiment too.

**Clairvoyance**

Sit and relax in a quiet room. Put something over your eyes and ears to block out sight and sound. Have a friend sit in another room and mentally send pictures to you. Don't try to do anything. Let whatever comes into your mind come in. Don't resist whatever comes in. You might want to record your impressions on a tape recorder while you're performing the experiment.

Compare the images you received with what your

friend sent. If you correctly described one or more of the pictures, it may be a sign of ESP.

Repeat the experiment with your friend as the receiver.

Here's another way to test your clairvoyance: Obtain twenty different picture poscards, each with a different scene on it. Have a friend place each postcard in a separate envelope and number the envelopes from 1 to 20. Then the envelopes should be sealed and shuffled.

Now have your friend hand you an envelope. You try to describe the scene on the postcard sealed inside the envelope. Your friend records which envelope (1 to 20) is being described along with the description you give.

Open the envelopes. See how closely the descriptions match the pictures on the postcards.

## Precognition

The simplest way to perform this experiment is to write down your dreams as soon as you wake up in the morning. Or try to wake yourself up from your dreams and write them down immediately. The important thing is to record your dreams right after waking. Otherwise, you'll probably forget them. A dream is like water being boiled—it evaporates quickly!

Notice times when your dreams seem more intense than usual. They could be ESP dreams strongly announcing themselves. Review your journal from time to time to see if any dreams came true.

## ESP Pet Tests

In Chapter 3, you read the story about Skippy and how he would wait for his master to return from school. It could be that Skippy learned through experience when the boy would come home. Or it could be ESP. If you have a dog who waits at home for your return from school, you can test it for ESP with this method devised by Zak Martin:

By varying your time of return by half an hour

to an hour, if possible, and by changing the vehicle in which you ride, you can make a good test. If your pet is waiting to meet you as before, or if a member of your family reports that your dog or cat has still shown its accustomed anticipatory [waiting] behavior, it may really be due to ESP.

What the heck—even if your pet doesn't pass the test, why not give it a treat for trying!

## PK Test

This test is an adaptation from one devised by authors Hans J. Eysenck and Carl Sargent. It will allow you to try your hand at PK by using a single six-sided die. You'll also need a glass or cup to shake it in, and a pen and paper to record your score.

Here's the procedure: When you toss the die, try to make each face of the die come up six times after you toss it. In other words, try to make the side with one dot come up six times, the side with two dots six times, and so on. Attempt to make the die land with the face you want up just by concentrating your mind on it.

It's best to toss the die against a hard surface such as a door or box. Since there are six faces on the die, you'll toss it thirty-six times. Record each result.

If you hit 11-12 times, that indicates some positive PK effect. Thirteen times is good, and more than fourteen hits is excellent.

# Books for Further Exploration

Michael Arvey particularly recommends the following books to readers who would like to learn more about ESP.

Doris Agee, *Edgar Cayce on ESP.* New York: Warner Books, 1969.

Loyd Auerbach, *ESP, Hauntings, and Poltergeists: A Parapsychologist's Handbook.* New York: Warner Books, Inc., 1986.

Hans J. Eysenck & Carl Sargent, *Explaining the Unexplained.* London: Multimedia Publications, Inc., 1982.

John Fairley & Simon Welfare, *Arthur C. Clarke's World of Strange Powers.* New York: G.P. Putnam's Sons, 1984.

Uri Geller, *My Story.* New York: Praeger Publishers, 1975.

Larry Kettelkamp, *Investigating Psychics: Five Life Histories.* New York: William Morrow & Co., 1977.

Zak Martin, *How To Develop Your ESP.* Great Britain: The Aquarian Press, 1986.

Jenny Randles, *Beyond Explanation?* Boston: Salem House, 1985.

# Additional Bibliography

Jan Ehrenwald, *The ESP Experience.* New York: Basic Books, Inc., 1978.

Kendrick Frazier, editor, *Science Confronts the Paranormal.* New York: Prometheus Books, 1986.

James Randi, *Flim-Flam: The Truth About Unicorns, Parapsychology, and Other Delusions.* New York: Lippincott and Crowell, Publishers, 1980.

Reader's Digest, *Into the Unknown.* New York: The Reader's Digest Association, Inc., 1982.

D. Scott Rogo, *Minds and Motion: The Riddle of Psychokinesis.* New York: Taplinger Publishing Co., Inc., 1986.

# Index

# Picture Credits

# About the Author

Michael Arvey is a freelance writer who has lived all over the U.S. He currently works as an editor and teaches correspondence courses in creative writing. At various times, he has also been a meditation instructor, message therapist, and poet.

Michael's interest in ESP comes from his own unexplained ESP experiences. He enjoys exploring the possibilities of this phenomenon.